the letters to the Thessalonians to life. This volume presents the reader with challenging and thought provoking insight into the relevant portions of Acts and the message to the fragile yet flourishing body of believers in Thessalonica.

Richard L. Ranger, PhD
Visiting Lecturer,
Uganda Christian University, Mukono

St. Paul wrote his letters to the believers in Thessalonica in order to instruct, encourage, and give them hope in a time of persecution. The Rev. Dr. Johannes W. H. van der Bijl's gift for narrative commentary, that first came to light in *Breakfast on the Beach,* now engages the imagination, mind, and heart of contemporary believers in this new, timely, and highly recommended retelling of 1 and 2 Thessalonians.

The Rt. Rev. Sean Semple
Bishop of Cyprus and the Gulf

1 & 2 THESSALONIANS

1 & 2 Thessalonians

A Life in Letters

Johannes W. H. van der Bijl

© 2025 Johannes W. H. van der Bijl

Published 2025 by Langham Global Library
An imprint of Langham Publishing
www.langhampublishing.org

Langham Publishing and its imprints are a ministry of Langham Partnership

Langham Partnership
PO Box 296, Carlisle, Cumbria, CA3 9WZ, UK
www.langham.org

ISBNs:
978-1-78641-096-2 Print
978-1-78641-106-8 ePub
978-1-78641-107-5 PDF

Johannes W. H. van der Bijl has asserted his right under the Copyright, Designs and Patents Act, 1988 to be identified as the Author of this work.

All rights reserved. No part of this publication may be reproduced, stored in a retrieval system or transmitted, in any form or by any means, electronic, mechanical, photocopying, recording or otherwise, without the prior written permission of the publisher or the Copyright Licensing Agency.

Requests to reuse content from Langham Publishing are processed through PLSclear. Please visit www.plsclear.com to complete your request.

All Scripture translations in this work, unless otherwise indicated, are the author's own.

Scripture quotations marked (ESV) are from The Holy Bible, English Standard Version® (ESV®), copyright © 2001 by Crossway, a publishing ministry of Good News Publishers. Used by permission. All rights reserved.

Scripture quotations marked (NIV) are taken from the Holy Bible, New International Version®, NIV®. Copyright © 1973, 1978, 1984, 2011 by Biblica, Inc.™ Used by permission of Zondervan.

British Library Cataloguing-in-Publication Data
A catalogue record for this book is available from the British Library

ISBN: 978-1-78641-096-2

Cover & Book Design: projectluz.com

Langham Partnership actively supports theological dialogue and an author's right to publish but does not necessarily endorse the views and opinions set forth here or in works referenced within this publication, nor can we guarantee technical and grammatical correctness. Langham Partnership does not accept any responsibility or liability to persons or property as a consequence of the reading, use or interpretation of its published content.

As someone who leads tours to the lands of the Bible for a living, I highly recommend this book. In an accessible and orderly way, van der Bijl brings to life what it was really like for Christians living in the first century. Focusing on Paul's journeys through Greece and his conversations with friends, especially as they relate to 1 and 2 Thessalonians and Acts, this book weaves together biblical knowledge with ancient history and engaging storytelling to offer a new and inviting way to study the world of the New Testament.

Derek Cooper, PhD
Managing Director,
Thomas Institute, Ireland

One disadvantage of the way we typically encounter the Bible is that we read or hear it in relatively small portions, so we miss the opportunity to gain an uncomplicated sense of the whole picture. *A Life in Letters* offers a broader, more connected, and engaging narrative that is easily missed in a regular diet of personal, group, or congregational Bible reflection on individual passages. It invites further reading and has reminded me in a new way of the witness of the early generations of Christian believers or, I should say, of the work of the Holy Spirit who called them to it.

This book presents the narrative as a novel, allowing the reader to "live" what is happening. Some characterization and a certain imaginative approach are present, to be sure. But the footnotes and comments referring to particular scriptures are designed to reduce the speculative aspect and encourage a direct dealing with the text that any commentary – even this narrative one – should be pleased to achieve.

Accessible to most readers, I would recommend this work to anyone seeking a better understanding of Paul and the early church, for whom it could provide a way into the Scriptures in general and the implications for faith in Jesus in particular.

Rev. Richard Crocker, PhD
Former General Secretary, EFAC

Johannes van der Bijl has the gift of not only seeing the truths of holy Scripture afresh but in assisting his readers to share in the encounter. When it comes to storytelling, as demonstrated in his two novels about Peter, *Breakfast on the Beach* and *For the Life of the World*, he is a master. In this book, and in his recent *Galatians: A Life in Letters*, van der Bijl combines the craft of storytelling with a conversational and accessible approach to unpacking theology. He also immerses himself in the historical and cultural context of the time and engages contemporary literature, tracing the use of words, phrases, and idiomatic speech to examine linguistic and conceptual connections. In doing so, van der Bijl enables his readers to grasp Paul's teachings in the setting of the relationships among Paul's fellow disciples and the society in which they lived. In other words, his readers "hear" the messages from Paul in the tradition of the first believers – and in a way that is almost in community with them. This narrative and teaching approach is most enriching and in his latest book, *1 & 2 Thessalonians: A Life in Letters*, it brings

Dedicated to the best mother-in-law
any man could ever wish for

Antje van Zyl/Coetzee (nee Wiersma),
affectionately known as "The Queen"

Mother to my wife, grandmother to my children,
great-grandmother to my grandchildren

30 July 1925–

We will always love you.

Contents

	Foreword xiii
	Acknowledgments xv
	Preface xvii
	Prologue..................................... xix
1	Challenging Crossroads........................... 1
2	The Misery of Misunderstanding................... 9
3	Learning Lessons and Discerning Directions........ 15
4	Setting Captives Free 29
5	Painful Gains – Power and Pain................... 43
6	Persecutors and Philosophers..................... 49
7	Encouragement and Exhortation.................. 59
8	Fear versus Faith................................ 71
9	Resistance and Assistance 91
10	Speculation, Signs, and Suffering.................. 99
11	Time to Travel................................. 115
	Short Biographies.............................. 123
	Timeline...................................... 149
	Appendix..................................... 153
	Bibliography 159

Foreword

The genre of a biblical commentary is all-too-familiar to students of the Bible – a reference book that helpfully explains the meaning of the biblical text but one that is typically done in a technical manner that is neither engaging nor inspiring. The narrative commentary on 1 & 2 Thessalonians by Johannes van der Bijl, however, is a decidedly different kind of reference book. Like a traditional commentary, it offers clear explanations of the biblical text – in this case explanations not just of Paul's two letters to the Thessalonians but also of the accounts in the book of Acts about the key events that lead up to the apostle's writing of these letters. Yet what is unique about this volume is the narrative style in which this explanation of the biblical text is given. Others, of course, including some gifted biblical scholars, have attempted to produce similar commentaries or books also written in a more conversational style. Yet writing in this narrative genre is not nearly as easy as it might seem and often results in dialogues that come across as stilted and forced. By contrast Johannes van der Bijl has produced a narrative of the biblical text that is natural, authentic and highly engaging. Furthermore, he does a commendable job in capturing for the modern reader the geographical setting, historical context and social world of New Testament times. I am confident that many will benefit and be edified by van der Bijl's narrative commentary on 1 and 2 Thessalonians.

Jeffrey A. D. Weima
Professor of New Testament
Calvin Theological Seminary, Michigan, USA

Acknowledgments

I once honestly forgot to acknowledge a Deacon in one of my thanksgiving messages at an Annual General Meeting, and his wife rivalled Mount Vesuvius in fury. Ever since then I have been nervous when the occasion comes to acknowledge the kindness and helpfulness of the many people who make my life and labour a pleasure. So, please know that I am grateful to all who have interacted with me over the years and who have been the iron that sharpens iron to me.

Having said that, I do wish to single out a few of these sharpeners who have played a major role in shaping this particular book.

The first and most obvious is God himself because without him I would not be who I am, and I would not be doing what I do. In him I truly live and move and have my being.

The second is my wife who enthusiastically shares my passion for uncovering things that illuminate what is written in the Scriptures. I believe I am one of the most spoilt husbands in the world.

The third is Dr. Jeff A. D. Weima, who is a relatively new acquaintance. His excitement about sharing his encyclopaedic knowledge as freely and forcefully as water gushing from a firehose is an inspiration. I devoured his commentary on 1 & 2 Thessalonians and then had the privilege of being a participant on a study tour following part of Paul's second missionary journey in Greece and Ephesus that was led by none other than the illustrious doctor himself. As I said to him at a dinner table with a view of the acropolis in Athens, I don't have many regrets in my life, but one of them is that I was never one of his students.

I am equally grateful to Christiana, our very well-informed local guide, and Christos, our expert bus driver, and Witte Tours for arranging this lifechanging tour.

Preface

> As with the previous volume, this book examines the life and ministry of Paul in a narrative style, weaving together the relevant texts from the book of Acts and from Paul's letters to the Thessalonians.

Our story begins in Corinth in the winter of AD 50, but then takes us back in time to examine the events in Paul's life and ministry starting with the Council of Jerusalem. We follow Paul back to Antioch, looking briefly at the events leading up to his choice of Silas as his partner for his second missionary journey. The story then continues as Paul visits various places in Asia, Macedonia, and Achaia, meets Timothy, Luke, and various other people along the way, and encounters serious opposition in Philippi, Thessalonica, and Berea before we finally return to his time in Corinth.

We are not told how Paul met fellow tentmakers Priscilla and Aquila, a converted Jewish couple based in Corinth who were there "because Claudius had commanded all Jews to leave Rome" (Acts 18:1–2), but more than likely, Paul needed employment and may have found them either in the town square or in the local synagogue. Luke tells us that Paul not only worked with this couple but also stayed with them. The two-storey shops in the marketplace would have had an upper room for the owners and their guests and a back room for employees.[1]

By the time Silas and Timothy returned from Macedonia, after their second trip there, Paul had already been active in the synagogues and, no doubt, also in the marketplace. However, thanks to the support sent to Paul from Philippi (Phil 4:15–16; see also 2 Cor 11:9), he was able to spend more time evangelizing. At some point during his lengthy stay in Corinth (Acts 18:11), Paul wrote two letters to the Christians at Thessalonica.

---

1. Bandy, *Apostle Paul*, 112. See also Mee and Spawforth, *Greece*, 149–57.

Prologue

Corinth (Acts 18:1–18), Winter AD 50

"Silas and Timothy have arrived," Aquila announced.

Paul had just returned from delivering an order for a tent he had completed early that morning, and he had a headache. The whereabouts and safety of his co-workers were always foremost on his mind.

"Thanks be to God," he said softly, raising his hands skyward.

"They are in the upper room," Priscilla said. "I hope you don't mind, but I told them to wash and rest first. They looked tired."

Then, seeing Paul's concerned expression, she quickly added, "Not tired as you were when you first came to us. No, they appear joyful and positive. It was just a long journey, as you know."

Paul breathed a sigh of relief. He thought back to the time when he had first arrived in Corinth. He had been exhausted and emotionally drained.[1] First, there had been the surprising spiritual struggle in Asia Minor, with the Holy Spirit himself blocking Paul as he tried to move forward . . . until he received, in a dream, an unmistakable direction to move on to Macedonia.[2] Then had come the astonishing arrest, beating,

---

1. 1 Corinthians 2:3.
2. Acts 16:6–10.

and imprisonment without trial in Philippi;[3] the disconcerting and dangerous threats in Thessalonica[4] and, later, in Berea;[5] the excessive idolatry in Athens that had greatly distressed him and the poor response to his teaching there;[6] the constant worry over the infant believers in all these cities as well as over the safety of Silas and Timothy who had returned there to encourage the believers;[7] and of course the hundreds of miles he himself had travelled, either walking or sailing, since leaving Antioch. By the time Paul arrived in Corinth, he had been spent on every level. But, thankfully, he had found believers in Corinth – men and women who had been brought to faith, he had later learned, by the ministry of Simon Peter and his wife on one of their first missions to Rome.[8]

"Then I will finish this stitching while they rest," Paul said, picking up some unfinished work as he sat down.

---

3. Acts 16:16–40.

4. Acts 17:5–10.

5. Acts 17:13–14.

6. Acts 17:16, 32–34.

7. 1 Thessalonians 3:1–10. Piecing together a few texts – 2 Corinthians 11:9, Philippians 4:14, and 1 Thessalonians 3:1 – suggests that Silas and Timothy were reunited with Paul in Athens at some point prior to his departure for Corinth and that Paul had then sent Silas back to Philippi (Silas brought the gift from Philippi) and Timothy to Thessalonica (1 Thessalonians 3:1–3). While it is possible that Silas and Timothy rejoined Paul in Athens, I have chosen to portray them as having been reunited in Corinth since 1 Thessalonians 3:6 seems to suggest that Paul's first letter to the Thessalonians appears to have been written from Corinth shortly after Timothy's return.

8. 1 Corinthians 1:12 seems to suggest that a faction in the Corinthian church claimed the supremacy of Peter.

It is possible that Peter had visited Corinth after Paul left or that others – like Priscilla and Aquila – had been forced out of Rome after having been converted to Christianity under the ministry of Peter.

"You have been working since before the rooster crowed this morning," Aquila stated flatly. "It is well past midday now. You also need to rest."

"I do not wish to be a burden to anyone,"[9] Paul said, almost absentmindedly, as he began to sew.

Aquila squatted in front of Paul and gently laid his hand on his friend's shoulder. "Paul," he said. "Look at me."

Paul raised his eyes to meet Aquila's gaze.

"You are no burden to us. You have proved that you are no idler."

Paul smiled a crooked smile and then, with a mischievous twinkle in his eye, said, "It is kind of you to say so, but it is my understanding that, under Roman law, while I may expect free lodging, I am not allowed to take advantage of the kind hospitality offered by the locals."[10]

"Ah! So, that's the problem, is it?" Priscilla exclaimed, throwing her hands in the air in an overdramatic gesture. Then, she quickly stepped closer to Paul and added in a low whisper, "I promise you, Paul, we will not report you to any Roman official!"

They all laughed. Ah, how grateful he was to be able to enjoy the company of mature followers of Jesus! And they, like

---

9. 1 Thessalonians 2:9.

10. See Nasrallah, *Archaeology*, 76–104. While the following inscription refers to government officials and their employees, it does give us a glimpse of what was considered socially acceptable behaviour for travellers: "Accommodation for all those who belong to my staff, for those on military service from all provinces, and for the freedmen and slaves of the excellent leader [Greek: the Augustus], and for their beasts, should be supplied free (ἄμισθον παρασχεθῆναι δεῖ), but in such a way that they do not demand the rest (of their costs) for no payment from those who are unwilling (to supply them) [gratuitam praestari oportet, ita ut reliqua ab invitis gratuita non exsigant]." Nasrallah, 95.

him, were tentmakers. Same Lord, same trade. What more could he ask for?

But Paul knew that he needed to rest, even though the repeated actions of laying out the woven goat-hair fabric,[11] shaping it according to the set pattern, and slowly stitching the various pieces together all helped him to relax and focus on something other than the strain of the ministry, the yearning to be teaching and training his new converts, and the anxiety he felt for the safety of his co-workers, especially young Timothy.

He looked down the cobbled street of the blazingly colourful and noisily busy town square and marketplace.[12] So many artisans from all over the world plying their wares so that they might provide for the needs of their families. He knew many of them by name. Every evening, after they laid down their tools and packed away their goods, Paul spoke to them about the Lord and the hope of eternity amid so many present uncertainties. Every Sabbath he reasoned with the Jews in the synagogue.[13] There was a growing interest, and some had already professed faith in Jesus. Few were wealthy or influential or even wise by human standards,[14] even though

---

11. Paul's hometown, Tarsus, was a city in the province of Cilicia. This province was famous for its Cilician fabric, which was a rough cloth made of goat hair, which was used primarily in tentmaking. Therefore, I have chosen this as the material of choice for Paul. Other possible materials used in tentmaking were leather and linen.

12. The Greek is *agora* which denotes an area that was much more than just a marketplace. It was a place where people could gather for social and public events as well as to buy various items such as food, clothing, and, in Paul's case, tents.

13. Acts 18:4.

14. 1 Corinthians 1:26.

many individuals in Corinth thought themselves wise.[15] They were just simple people who lived in abject fear of unpredictable and impulsive gods, ominous omens, and chilling curses. For this reason, the area was filled with various temples, shrines, sacred spaces, and sacred fountains.[16]

The gospel promised them freedom from this daily sense of dread. It gave them hope. Paul felt a burning urgency to tell them that they no longer needed to flounder hopelessly in a turbulent sea of falsehood. He had unwittingly and, in some sense, unwillingly stumbled on the "cure" for the deadliest disease of all – sin – and he wasn't about to keep this good news to himself. Such freedom was to be shared, not stored.

"Here," Priscilla said, breaking his train of thought. "Drink some of this barley water. I put a sprig of mint in it. It is wholesome and refreshing.[17] And have a few dates and nuts. Look at you! You are wasting away before my eyes."

Paul smiled as he gulped down a mouthful. Then he sighed. Priscilla was right. The warm liquid was soothing, and he felt his weariness subside.

"Now, why don't you go lie down at the back and let us take care of business, hmm?"[18]

---

15. The Athenian statesman Aristides (530–468 BC) asserted that on every street in Corinth one met a so-called wise man who had his own solutions to humanity's problems. *Archaeological Study Bible*, 1865, note on 1:19.

16. Mee and Spawforth, *Greece*, 149–57.

17. Joshua J. Mark, "Kykeon," *World History Encyclopedia*, 2 September 2009, https://www.worldhistory.org/Kykeon/.

18. Each two-storey shop (2.7–3.6 metres wide, 3.6 metres deep, and 4 metres high, with a doorway that was 2.5 metres wide) in the marketplace would have had an upper room for the owners and their guests and a back room for employees. Bandy, *Apostle Paul*, 112. See also Mee and Spawforth, *Greece*, 149–57.

"You are right, Priscilla," Paul agreed reluctantly, grabbing a handful of dates and nuts and popping a few in his mouth. "A quick rest will be of benefit to me, but do be sure to wake me as soon as Timothy and Silas are up. It will be like the balm of Gilead[19] for me to speak with them."

"Go," she said, shooing him off like a small child. "I will call you when it is time."

Paul stretched and then shuffled to the back of the little shop that they shared. He rolled out his sleeping mat, removed his sandals, and laid his head on a bundle of goat-hair fabric. As he closed his eyes he thanked God for his many blessings, especially for Priscilla and Aquila. He was truly grateful for his new friends.

"I am awake, Aquila," Paul said through a yawn, shuffling sleepily back into the shop, rubbing his eyes with his hand. "No need to hush young Timothy, even though he does make more noise than a cantankerous camel in the evening!"

"Paul!" cried Timothy, pushing through the group and rushing to embrace the man he loved as a father. The two men, one older and the other younger, laughed and wept in each other's arms.

"It does me good to see you, my son,"[20] Paul said at last, still holding him by the forearms while looking inquiringly into his beloved disciple's eyes.

"I bring greetings from the believers in Thessalonica," Timothy said.

---

19. Jeremiah 8:22; see also Genesis 37:25.
20. 1 Timothy 1:2.

"And I bring yet another generous gift from the believers in Philippi,"[21] said Silas, stepping forward to greet Paul and displaying what he held in his hands.[22]

"Oh, thanks be to God!" Paul exclaimed as he embraced Silas, kissing him on both cheeks. "What a joy to see you, Silas! Both of you, safe and sound."

The three men embraced and praised God together in joyful prayer and song.

"And this!" Paul said, breaking the embrace and looking at the gift. "This wonderful gift will free me up to devote all my time to the ministry I have been called to do!"

"And," Silas added, "unlike their unbelieving neighbours, they do not wish to be honoured or thanked or even praised for their gifts, generous as they are."[23]

"True," Timothy said, smiling. "They know that kindness to those in need is rewarded by the Lord."[24] Then he became serious. "Paul, you need to know that there has been conflict in Thessalonica."

"And our brethren?" Paul asked, concerned. "Are they unsettled by these trials?"

"No," Timothy replied. "No, to the contrary, their faith and love have deepened,[25] and they are bold in speaking to their unbelieving neighbours about the good news of Jesus."[26]

---

21. According to Philippians 4:15–16, the church in Philippi sent financial aid to Paul at least twice during his stay in Thessalonica. See Weima, *1–2 Thessalonians*, 26.

22. 2 Corinthians 11:9; Philippians 4:15.

23. For a very interesting study on the societal understanding of gift-giving in the first century AD, see Peterman, *Paul's Gift from Philippi*.

24. Proverbs 19:17.

25. 1 Thessalonians 3:6.

26. 1 Thessalonians 1:7–8.

"Yes, I had warned them that all who seek to live godly lives will be persecuted.[27] That is why I sent you to them."[28]

"But there are several unbelievers in the city who are troubling them with false statements about you . . . and the brethren themselves have pressing questions about some of their members who have died since you were with them. I think they may be confused as to their destiny. They have had to reconsider and revise their old views on life and death. Our manner of grieving is so different from those who have no hope of eternal life."[29]

"Yes, we will have to write to them – and soon. Perhaps even this evening."

"I have all the necessary writing materials, Paul," Aquila said enthusiastically, handing them each a tumbler of barley water.

"And I have all the necessary ingredients for a wholesome meal for you all," Priscilla said, returning from the market with a basket laden with fresh produce as well as dried fruit and fish.

"Thank you!" Timothy exclaimed, looking eagerly at the food. "I'm famished!"

"You're always famished," Silas laughed.

"Leave him alone," fussed Priscilla, "all young men are constantly in dire need of good nourishment!"

"In dire need, is he?" Paul echoed. "Then we should eat first. Come, my son, tell me all I need to know about our brethren in Thessalonica."

Paul sat in the window, gazing up into the night sky's inky blackness punctured by an innumerable number of stars. "Look

---

27. 2 Timothy 3:12.
28. 1 Thessalonians 3:4.
29. 1 Thessalonians 4:13.

up at the stars," God had said to Abraham. "Count them if you are able. So shall your descendants be."[30] This promise of a global family of Abraham was being fulfilled in Paul's lifetime. The gospel was being taken into the whole world.

Paul couldn't help wondering what Abraham would have thought of his ministry to all the nations. What would the prophets have thought? Those who reflected on this promise of global blessing believed that the nations were to come to Jerusalem, not the reverse. But then they could not have known that a heavenly Jerusalem would displace the earthly one . . . a Jerusalem that would not be confined by geographical location.

Like the mobile throne Ezekiel saw in his bizarre vision while in enemy territory, God was not restricted to a physical building in Judea.[31] Besides, did Jesus not clearly teach that he was the tabernacle . . . that he was the temple[32] and that those who believed in him were filled with the glorious divine presence? In that case, the temple was wherever believers gathered,[33] which meant that the nations were in fact coming to Jerusalem, just not exactly in the way they had thought.

"Paul?"

He turned to face his beloved disciple, Timothy, who handed him a tumbler of warm milk.

"The Lord has added more to our flock," Paul said.

"Yes," Timothy said, sipping his own drink. "But they are all so different, aren't they?"

"True, there are so many different people from so many different parts of the world in Corinth! They each bring with them their own cultures and beliefs. And they are also from

---

30. Genesis 15:5.
31. Ezekiel 1:1–3:15.
32. John 1:14; 2:18–22; 14:23; Ephesians 2:19–22; Revelation 21:22.
33. Matthew 18:20.

different levels in society. I am afraid that these differences may one day prove to be a challenge to unity in the group."[34]

Silas joined them. "You have been busy, Paul," he said.

"The Spirit has been busy, you mean. I am only the messenger. It is God who prepares and opens hearts, remember?"

"True, but a messenger who brings the message clearly and delivers it persuasively. That man over there tells me he used to be engaged in sexual relationships with other men. But now, after hearing you speak about purity in the Lord, he has left that lifestyle altogether."

"Oh, Silas, there are several previously sexually immoral people here this evening, not just men in sexual relationships with other men," Timothy remarked.

"Yes," Paul added. "Also, ex-thieves, drunkards, adulterers, hedonists, and idolaters. But now, all washed, sanctified, and justified in the name of the Lord Jesus Christ and by the Spirit of our God."[35]

"So, the answer to the prophet Jeremiah's question, 'Can an Ethiopian change his skin or a leopard its spots?'[36] is clearly not 'no,'" Silas responded.

"With God, all things are possible," Paul replied, smiling.[37]

"And the Jews here?" Timothy asked. "Are they open to the message of Jesus?"

Paul sighed. "Not all of them. This problem has dogged my steps ever since we first left Antioch."

"Yes," Silas added, "even when we were at the Council in Jerusalem there were those who opposed you."

"The Council in Jerusalem," Paul said softly, almost to himself. "It feels like a lifetime has passed since then."

---

34. 1 Corinthians 1:10–13.
35. 1 Corinthians 6:9–11.
36. Jeremiah 13:23.
37. Matthew 19:26.

1

Challenging Crossroads

On the Road to and from Jerusalem (Acts 15:1–35)

> Paul and Barnabas travel from Antioch to Jerusalem to attend a council to discuss the issue of circumcision for gentile believers. The chapter also explores the relationship and the tensions that arise between Paul, Barnabas, and John Mark.

"You can't just expect people to change their thinking overnight, Paul," Barnabas insisted as they walked from Antioch to Jerusalem.

"Why not?" Paul shot back. "I did."

"That's true, but only after Jesus dramatically confronted you face to face on the road to Damascus. None of these people have had such a heavenly visitation."

"But we all study the same Scriptures, don't we? We all pray for enlightenment and guidance from the Holy Spirit. Surely, his word and his Spirit are as good as any vision or supernatural appearance?"

"That is true. However, the Spirit who inspired and illuminates the word is patient and gracious and gentle and loving and kind. Our God is a shepherd who leads his lambs gently.[1] Think of his patience with our forebears in the wilderness."

"And look what happened to them . . ."

"Paul!" Barnabas stopped walking, exasperated.

Paul turned, a perplexed look on his face. "What?"

"You must allow the Holy Spirit to change the hearts of our brethren in his time. It takes more than persuasive words and logic. You are challenging years of deep-rooted teaching and learning and believing."

"Barnabas, I'm not sure you understand the gravity of the situation," Paul replied, untying a skin of water and taking a quick drink. "We are standing at a crossroads. We must persuade them to take a different course or our mission to the Gentiles will end abruptly."

"But changing course is challenging . . . it is not easy. Remember, Peter . . . and me?"[2]

Paul winced. Yes, he remembered. He would seek Peter out as soon as they arrived and apologize for his heavy-handedness in Antioch.

"Besides," Barnabas continued, "rumour has it that some of the Zealots suspect anyone who associates with Gentiles as being collaborators with Rome. The influx of uncircumcised believers in Caesarea and Antioch has placed some of our brethren in Jerusalem in a very difficult position."[3]

"What do you mean?" Paul asked, frowning.

"They are afraid, Paul, and rightly so."

---

1. Isaiah 40:11.
2. Galatians 2:11–14.
3. Schnabel, *Early Christian Mission*, 1009–10.

"So, to save their own skins, they want us to demand that the Gentiles be circumcised. But it won't stop there, Barnabas, I can assure you. These are Pharisees, remember? They will want the Gentiles to observe not only the law but the law as they interpret it. I was one of them, in case you have forgotten. I know how they think."

"I am just asking that you try to understand their predicament," Barnabas said testily. "Things are not as clear as you may think they are."

Paul looked at his friend. Barnabas had believed in him when no one else did. Was that part of the problem for Paul? Did he harbour some hidden resentment in his heart towards those who had not believed in him at first and then challenged him later on? Pride was such a subtle menace.

"Barnabas," Paul said soberly, "one of the first things I want to do when we get to Jerusalem is to apologize to Peter. Humbling myself before him will be good practice for me to humble myself before the council."

"And what about my cousin?" Barnabas asked pointedly.[4]

Paul tilted his head slightly and looked at Barnabas with raised eyebrows. Then he snorted, turned on his heel, and walked on.

"What about forgiving as you have been forgiven? Have you thought about that?" Barnabas yelled.

Paul flung his hands in the air but continued to walk in silence.

---

4. For an in-depth study on a possible explanation for why John Mark abandoned Paul and Barnabas in Perga and for Paul's subsequent refusal to take him on the second journey, see Valdez, *Shores of Perga*. Also see van der Bijl, *Galatians*, 13–14.

"Are you happy with the outcome of the council?"[5] Barnabas asked as they walked out through the gates of Jerusalem on their way back to Antioch.

"Yes," Paul said, a big grin on his face. "Very happy."

As they walked on, the small delegation[6] paused to glance briefly at the place where the crucifixion and resurrection had taken place.

"It is amazing to think of all that has happened since Jesus told his first followers to make disciples of all the nations, don't you think?" Paul said thoughtfully.

Silas smiled. "I think the first disciples thought he was going to restore the kingdom to Israel,"[7] he said. "They would never have imagined that being witnesses to Jesus to the ends of the earth would include Gentiles."

"Yes," Judas laughed. "I think even now some struggle with the idea of a kingdom not restrained by borders defined in the law, whether geographic or ethnic."

"Well," replied Paul, "until I met Jesus on the road to Damscus, I would not have even considered the possibility. It really is amazing how blind I was. It's like I had a veil pulled over my eyes. But it's all right there in the very law I thought I knew so well. Abraham's descendants were meant to be a blessing to

---

5. For a narrative account of the Jerusalem Council, see van der Bijl, *Life of the World*, 151–62.

6. According to Acts 15:22–29, Judas – who was called Barsabbas – and Silas accompanied Paul and Barnabas as witnesses from the Jerusalem Council. However, it is possible that they are the only named delegates and that an unnamed number of individuals accompanied them. In Acts 15:36–41, it seems that Silas and John Mark were present in Antioch after the Jerusalem delegation had returned to Jerusalem (Acts 15:33–35). While it is possible that Silas had returned with John Mark "some time later" (see Acts 15:36), it is equally plausible that John Mark was part of the original delegation and that the two had remained in Antioch after the rest had left.

7. Acts 1:6.

all nations, not just one.[8] And even when Israel was in Egypt, God sent the plagues so that the Egyptians might know him and that his name might be proclaimed over all the earth.[9] In fact, God tells us in Deuteronomy that our very obedience to his law was to demonstrate his righteous presence with us!"[10]

"Not to mention all the references to the Messiah being a light to the nations in Isaiah's prophecies," Barnabas added.[11]

"And what about Naaman the Syrian?" Judas asked. "Wasn't that miracle a witness to the Gentiles?"[12]

"Don't forget about Jonah," Silas chimed in enthusiastically. "He wanted the enemies of Israel to be judged, but God wanted to save them!"[13]

"Why were you two so quiet at the council?" Paul asked jokingly.

"Not everyone is as eloquent as you, Paul," Judas replied.

"So, I'm the eloquent one now, am I?" Paul laughed. "I've always been told that the eloquent one is Barnabas!"

Judas turned to John Mark, who seemed to be trying hard to remain inconspicuous among the other delegates. "Talking about being quiet . . . why are you so quiet, young John Mark?"

"I have nothing to say," Mark replied, glancing nervously at Paul.

"Indeed!" Paul snorted. "Best to remember that."

There was an awkward silence as Paul turned on his heel and marched off.

"What was that about?" Judas asked.

---

8. Genesis 12:1–3.
9. Exodus 9:14, 16.
10. Deuteronomy 4:5–8.
11. Isaiah 42:6; 49:6; 52:10; 60:3.
12. 2 Kings 5:1–19.
13. Jonah 4:10–11.

Silas shook his head. "Some things are better left alone, Judas."

"But..."

"Just let it go. Please. For Mark's sake if not ours."

Barnabas looked at Mark's ashen face, then spun around and hurried after Paul.

"Paul," he called out, a little more harshly than he had intended, "you spoke with Peter, but did you speak to John Mark?"

"He has been avoiding me ever since we arrived in Jerusalem," Paul said without stopping or turning to face his friend.

"Do you blame him?" Barnabas shot back, catching up with Paul. "He's terrified of you, and rightly so. Your angry outburst in Perga left a very negative impression on him.[14] In fact, I believe he has been avoiding me, too, because he thinks I agree with you... but I don't."

Paul stopped abruptly and turned to face Barnabas. "We have wonderful news to deliver to our brethren in Antioch. So, I suggest we get on with our journey and discuss this later."

"You can't hold on to your anger forever."

"Anger? I am not angry with your cousin, Barnabas. I just don't trust him anymore."

"Trust? Is it a matter of trust, Paul, or is it perhaps that your pride was wounded when he challenged you in Perga?"

"Barnabas!" Paul almost shouted. "I have said that we can discuss this at another time, not now. Now come, we have a long journey ahead of us."

With that, he turned around and walked on.

---

14. For a discussion on what might have caused John Mark to leave the group, see van der Bijl, *Galatians*, 13–14.

Barnabas looked at the rest of the group. While the others looked confused and bewildered, John Mark looked like a frightened rabbit. Silas locked eyes with Barnabas and shook his head as if to indicate that this was not the time to press the matter any further.

Did Silas know something that he did not? Barnabas wondered. Perhaps John Mark had felt that he could confide in Silas as a neutral party.

But as Paul had said, they still had far to go. So, it was best to get on.

2

The Misery of Misunderstanding

Antioch (Acts 15:30–40), Spring AD 49

> Paul and Barnabas return to Antioch and deliver the Jerusalem Council's decision to the believers there. It also explores the disagreement between Paul and Barnabas over the matter of taking John Mark with them on their next journey – a disagreement that leads, ultimately, to their separation.

The delegation delivered the letter to the believers in Antioch, and Judas and Silas spent some time encouraging and strengthening these ethnically diverse believers. Most of the Jerusalem contingent had left, but Silas and John Mark decided to stay on.[1] It seemed to Mark that Paul was so busy teaching

---

1. Silas might have stayed in Antioch or left with the Jerusalem delegation and then either returned soon after or when he was summoned by Paul to join the apostle on his missionary journey in place of Barnabas. For

and preaching that he hardly knew that Mark existed. Even so, he tried to stay out of Paul's way as much as possible. Other than running errands for his cousin, Mark continued to copy his notes on Peter's teaching.[2] He decided to make copies for all the communities. But he did not tell anyone in Antioch what he was doing, not even Barnabas. Only Silas knew.

On several occasions, Barnabas tried to reason with Paul about his attitude towards Mark, but Paul shut him down every single time. Several others also urged Paul to be reconciled with Mark, but he resisted, insisting that they did not understand the situation. Barnabas had tried to talk to Mark, too, but the young man was evasive and simply said he preferred not to raise the issue again for fear of an argument. This bothered Barnabas as he felt he was being torn in two. He just could not understand why they could not move on.

But one evening, as they all sat in the courtyard under a dazzling spring sky, talking about the remarkable numerical and spiritual growth of the community in Antioch, Paul suddenly turned to Barnabas, saying, "Why don't you and I return and visit all the communities we established and see how they are doing?"

There was an abrupt lull in the conversation as everyone waited, eager to hear Barnabas's reply.

Barnabas looked at Mark. Out of the corner of his eye, he saw Silas shaking his head as if to say that this was not the moment. But Barnabas felt, deep in this heart, that this situation had gone on long enough.

"I think that's a wonderful idea, Paul. It will be a good opportunity for you and Mark to mend your broken relationship."

---

the purpose of this narrative, I have chosen to depict Silas as having stayed on in Antioch.

2. See van der Bijl, *Life of the World*, 74–75, 125–28.

"That's not . . . what I mean to say is . . . that is . . ." Paul spluttered, totally taken by surprise. Then, regaining his equanimity he stated emphatically, "No. That's not a good idea at all. And this is not a good time to discuss the matter, not in front of everyone here."

"Why? For a long time now I have tried to reason with you about this embarrassing division in our community. I know others present here have spoken to you about this also. But you have refused to listen to any of us. So, as Jesus taught us, I am bringing up the matter before those in leadership here."[3]

"Cousin," Mark pleaded.

"Barnabas, you don't know the whole story," Silas said.

"No? Well, then, maybe now is a good time to hear the whole story," Paul thundered. "Go on," he shouted at Mark, "tell them why you ran back home to your mother when you should have been faithful to our cause."[4]

Mark was visibly trembling at this unexpected outburst. The others all stared at Paul in shock. Where did this anger come from?

"What's the problem, young man?" Paul demanded. "Why not admit that you told them in Jerusalem that I did not demand that Sergius Paulus be circumcised."

"That's not what happened," Mark blurted out, his voice cracking.

"No?" Paul yelled back.

"Let him speak, Paul," Barnabas insisted.

"Why?" Paul erupted once again. "Surely you don't think it was pure coincidence that after your cousin returned home,

---

3. Matthew 18:15–17.

4. The Greek word used to describe the "sharp disagreement" between Paul and Barnabas is *paroxumos*, a very strong word that could be translated as "paroxysm," "seizure," "explosion," or "eruption."

those troublemakers from Jerusalem went and confused our brethren in Galatia, do you?"

"I didn't . . ." Mark began timidly.

"You didn't what?" Paul interrupted. "Speak up, man. Tell the whole assembly how you betrayed us."

Shock waves rippled audibly through the group. Mark shook his head, tears flowing freely. Then he stood up and fled.

"Paul!" Barnabas spoke through clenched teeth, veins bulging in his neck, his rage clearly visible on his face. "How dare you accuse him of betrayal!"

"Your cousin is both a traitor and a coward!" Paul shot back. "Once again, he has run away with his tail between his legs. He can't even defend himself because there is no defence for treachery!"

Manaen stood up. "Paul, we need to discuss this matter calmly and rationally."

"Calmly?" Paul jumped up. "You tell me to be calm? For months now, I have struggled to undo what that young man did! You read that letter from our Galatian brethren . . . you saw the damage inflicted on them because of those legalists. They very nearly embraced a distorted gospel! Mark was vindictive! He was angry with me and so he . . ."

"Paul," Silas interrupted, his voice raised to make himself heard, "don't say anything now that you will regret later."

"Regret!" Paul shrieked, his voice rising in waves, his hands flailing in the air. "Regret? The only regret I have is that we took him along with us in the first place!"

"Paul . . ." Lucius held his hands out as if to calm Paul down.

"And now you!" Paul spun around and jabbed a finger into Barnabas's chest. "You want me to take him with us again? Why? So that he can create more havoc?"

"Yes!" Barnabas pushed Paul back roughly and advanced until their faces almost touched. "Yes, I want him to go with us.

I want him to go with us because I think everyone deserves a second chance . . . even though I don't believe you are right in your monstrous accusations. I don't know where you get your information from, but you have no proof that what you think of my cousin is true!"

"Brothers," Niger said coming between them. "This is no way to solve . . ."

"No!" Paul snapped, beside himself with fury. "I will not be called a liar!"

"This is unreasonable, Paul," Niger said, trying once more to calm them down. "No one has accused you of being a liar."

"He has," Paul yelled, pointing at Barnabas. "He believes his wretched cousin rather than me! I will not take him with me even if he was the last man standing."

"Very well," Barnabas said, standing back and smoothing out his garment, having regained his composure. "Then I will not go with you either."

"You don't mean that . . ." Paul spluttered, suddenly sensing that he had pushed Barnabas too far.

"I do," Barnabas replied quietly but stiffly. "I will take Mark with me to Cyprus. We will leave with the first ship out." Barnabas walked out of the courtyard in search of his cousin.

3

Learning Lessons and Discerning Directions

Travelling to Macedonia (Acts 15:41; 16:1–10)

> Paul, now accompanied by Silas, travels through Syria and Cilicia, strengthening the churches. They then travel to Derbe and Lystra, where they meet Timothy, who joins them on their journey. The chapter also explores Paul's dream of a man from Macedonia, which leads them to journey to Philippi.

Barnabas and John Mark had left for Cyprus the week before. Now the brothers laid hands on Paul and Silas and commended them to the grace of the Lord for the journey they were about to undertake.

The mood in Antioch was still quite sombre after the sharp exchange between Barnabas and Paul. Paul had not joined the rest when they went to the harbour. He felt that he had said his piece and was justified in his decision regarding Mark.

After the initial chorus of goodbyes, Paul and Silas walked in silence for a long while, both seemingly lost in their own thoughts. Then, without stopping, Silas suddenly said, "You were wrong about John Mark, you know."

Paul sighed. "Oh Silas," he said, his feet suddenly feeling like lead, "I really don't want to talk about that."

"Good, because if you don't talk, then you will listen better to what I have to say."

Paul stopped to look at his new companion. He had not experienced Silas being so direct before.

Silas turned and faced Paul. "Mark didn't speak to anyone in Jerusalem except to me."

For a moment the only sounds heard were the birds and the cicadas.

Paul's mouth felt as though it had turned into a sandpit. "What?" he rasped.

"Let me finish before you say anything more. I told you the other night that you would regret your angry words, and believe me you will by the time I've told you the truth of the matter."

Silas took a deep breath and then continued. "It was his silence that made them suspicious. Of course, they knew Mark had spoken to me, and so they asked me to repeat what he had told me, but as he had spoken to me in confidence, I also said nothing. That was why they went to Pisidian Antioch."

Paul suddenly felt faint. "You mean . . . ?"

"Yes, Mark was loyal to you. It was his loyalty to you that made them suspect that you were doing something they would not condone, and so they went to see for themselves."

"Why . . . why didn't he . . . why didn't *you* say something?"

"It was not my story to tell, and as for Mark not telling you – well, you did a good job avoiding him or shutting him up whenever he tried to say anything. In short, Paul – forgive me – but you were wrong, and you owe that young man, not to mention Barnabas, an apology. You don't seem able to see another side to the story other than your own. That really is something you need to work on."

Paul saw a rock by the side of the road and went over to it. He sat down heavily, his head in his hands.

"I don't owe him an apology," he said softly.

"Excuse me?" Silas was about to object when Paul continued.

"I don't owe him an apology – I owe him much more than that. I have sinned against him publicly and accused him unjustly. I must repent. I must beg his forgiveness."[1]

Silas breathed a sigh of relief. "Here, drink some water. I have more to tell you."

"More? Oh, Father in Heaven, forgive your foolish child. I have once more allowed my pride and my anger to cloud my judgement." He gulped down the water and then poured some into his hands to wash his face.

"Here in my bag, I have several copies of notes Mark has rewritten from lectures given by Peter a few years ago."

"Lectures?" Paul felt quite ill. How could he have been so wrong about this young man?

"Yes, lectures. Mark was one of Peter's first disciples in Jerusalem and a very astute one at that. He took copious notes of all that Peter taught. Then, together with Peter and others, including me, he rewrote them in a more coherent form. And he has been making copies of his notes to distribute among our communities."

---

1. I believe that Paul would have followed his own advice – as given in Ephesians 4:26–27 – and reconciled sooner rather than later. Since he speaks highly of both Barnabas and Mark in later letters – see 1 Corinthians 9:5–6, Colossians 4:10, and 2 Timothy 4:11 – I think it likely that this rift was healed fairly soon after the split.

"So that was what he was doing when he sat alone in the corner of the courtyard. And I thought he was just avoiding work."

"No, he was writing out a copy to leave with Niger. Paul, permit me to say that you allowed your misguided and unfounded judgement on what you thought to be Mark's behaviour to cloud everything you thought about him."

"Steady on, Silas, I feel guilty enough already."

"And so you should, Paul. You could have scarred that young man for life. I am just thankful that Barnabas did not side with you. That was what Mark thought, and that is why he never spoke to Barnabas about this matter. He believed that as Barnabas had sided with you in Perga, he was still of the same opinion.[2] You very nearly broke up a beautiful family relationship."

"Oh, Silas." Paul looked up at him piteously. "I must write to them immediately. I must beg them to forgive me."

"We can write to them soon, Paul, perhaps once we get to Tarsus. But first, take a look at Mark's notes."

Paul gingerly took the scroll from Silas and unrolled it. "The beginning of the gospel of Jesus Christ, the Son of God," he read out loud. His eyes darted from line to line across the parchment, hardly believing what he was reading. Then the tears began to flow, and he wept miserably.

At their next place of rest, Paul wrote a letter of heartfelt regret and had it taken by courier to Salamis, where he knew Barnabas still had family connections. Having been able to deal with his

---

2. Walker, *Steps of Saint Paul*, 70–71.

anger and his guilt energized him, and he felt as if a weight had been removed from his shoulders.[3]

Paul and Silas busied themselves going from community to community, many of which Paul had established years ago,[4] encouraging the brethren and telling them of the outcome of the Jerusalem Council. Then they pressed on up the pass through the Taurus Mountains and the stunningly beautiful gorge known as the Cilician Gates towards Derbe and Lystra.

On their arrival in Lystra, after having visited with several brethren in Derbe, they found that Barnabas had sent a reply to Paul's letter to Timothy's household. All was well. Mark had told his cousin the truth even before they arrived in Cyprus, and so the rift was healed from all sides. Lois had detained the bearer of the letter as she had wisely and correctly assumed that Paul would want to reply immediately.

After another hearty meal served by their hosts, Paul took Silas to the spot where the incident that nearly cost him his life had taken place.[5]

"It was my fault," Paul said. "I should have known that the Lycaonians would misinterpret the miracle. What else were they supposed to think except that we were their gods in human form?"

"That's the problem with signs and wonders," Silas agreed. "They are open to any number of interpretations depending on the perspective of those involved."

---

[3]. Psalm 32:1–5.

[4]. For his safety, Paul returned to Tarsus from Jerusalem (Acts 9:30). About ten years later, Barnabas went to Tarsus to find Paul and to bring him to Antioch (Acts 11:25). Galatians 1:18 and 2:1 suggest that Paul's early ministry activities lasted for about 14 years, during which he most likely planted several churches in Syria and Cilicia.

[5]. Acts 14:19–20.

"But Timothy was in that same crowd, and because he understood what I was saying, he believed."[6]

"Yes, his presence was advantageous, wasn't it?"

"Advantageous? He was a gift sent from heaven. He helped Barnabas and the others half-carry me to their home, where Eunice and Lois made sure I was fit to leave the next day."[7]

"And they believed too?"

"Yes. But unlike their fellow townsfolk, they knew the Scriptures well, and they had made sure Timothy understood and believed the faith despite his father being a Greek."

"You are very fond of this young man, aren't you?"

Paul sighed as he bent down to pick up a rock that might very well have been one of those that had been thrown at him so many years ago.

"You know, as a Pharisee, I was expected to marry. I wanted to, believe me, but my studies always came first, above all else."

"Your parents made no arrangements?"

"Oh, arrangements were made alright, but I never followed through.[8] And once I had become a follower of the Way, of course, it was over. But my point is, if I had married, I would very much have liked to have had a son like young Timothy."

"He seems to have latched on to you as if you were his father."

"Well, that's quite understandable. His father died when he was very young."[9]

---

6. This is speculation on my part.

7. This is speculation on my part.

8. This is speculation on my part.

9. As Timothy's father is only mentioned in passing in Acts 16:1–3 – with reference to his ethnicity – and since only Lois and Eunice appear to have been instrumental in Timothy's education from his childhood – 2 Timothy 1:5; 3:14–15 – I am assuming that Timothy's father was probably dead by the time Paul came to Lystra. The fact that Timothy and his mother were

"He is a remarkable young man. The brethren from Lystra and Iconium speak very highly of him."

"Yes, he has memorized most of the sacred writings and can be very persuasive in his defence of the faith."

"There is a problem, though . . . you do know that, right? Timothy spends much time in the small gymnasium here, and everyone has seen him there."[10]

"Yes, I understand what you are getting at Silas. He is not circumcised."

"I wouldn't have mentioned it except that I know this might be a problem for us when we try to access synagogues further along."

Paul couldn't help laughing. "You don't have to be so cautious in addressing this issue, Silas. You know that despite my resistance to Gentiles being forced to submit to Jewish rituals and rites, I'm not opposed to Jewish men being circumcised."

"So, you are not against him being circumcised?"

"No, I'm not. Timothy is not Titus.[11] In fact, I will circumcise him myself, if he will let me."

"That will delay our departure for at least three days."

"Let's give him four, shall we?"

"I hope you have a steady hand, Paul."

"Are you sure you are alright?" Paul asked Timothy as they continued their journey northwards from Pisidian Antioch.

---

living with her mother (that is, his grandmother) may be taken as a further indication that the men in the family were no longer alive.

10. Timothy seems to have been concerned with bodily exercise (1 Timothy 4:8) and, in those times, it was customary for athletes to train in the nude.

11. Galatians 2:3–5.

"It's been weeks now, Paul! I'm not a baby, you know!" Timothy laughed. "But thank you for asking."

"If only you *were* a baby," Silas remarked. "Circumcision on adults can be a killer."

"You exaggerate," Timothy chuckled.

"No, really. Remember what happened to Shechem and his brethren?"[12]

Paul burst out laughing. "Where on earth do you get that awful sense of humour from?"

"I'll have you know I worked long and hard on learning how to be funny. My family was always too serious for my liking."

"Well, maybe you should work a little longer and a little harder," Timothy blurted out without thinking. Then he blushed, a deep shade of red. "I'm so sorry. I didn't mean to be disrespectful at all. I know I am still very young and ought to respect my elders."

"And so you should, young man," said Silas, in a deep and overly dramatic voice. "Whenever you find them!"

"Timothy, he's just teasing you," said Paul, putting his hand on Timothy's shoulder. "You are as entitled to a bit of levity as we are. And believe me, a sense of humour comes in handy at times like these."

"What do you mean 'at times like these'? Are we in trouble?" Timothy sounded concerned.

"Not trouble exactly," Paul spoke slowly. "I'm just not sure where we are supposed to be going. Every time I try to go in a certain direction, I sense that the Holy Spirit prevents us from going there. Not Asia, nor Bithynia. That's why we are pressing on westwards."

---

12. Genesis 34:14–29.

"But how do you know that it is the Holy Spirit who is preventing us?" Timothy inquired. "Do you hear him speaking to you?"

"Well, the Holy Spirit speaks in various ways," Paul replied. "At times he speaks directly through a prophet, like a man named Agabus who once foretold a worldwide famine.[13] Other times, he speaks through the wisdom of another person or through a vision or dream. But most of the time, he speaks to me in my spirit."

"What does that mean?"

"It means that I sense a very strong impression that I should do this or not do that."

"But how do you know that it is the Spirit of Jesus and not some evil spirit?"

"Ah, yes, a very good question, my son." Paul turned and earnestly looked Timothy in the eyes. "As a follower of Jesus, you will know the difference between the two just as you know the difference between a loving parent and an enemy, or, to use the words of Jesus, you will know the difference between the voice of the shepherd and the voice of the stranger.[14] Always remember, the enemy may masquerade as an angel of light,[15] but if you are walking in step with the Spirit, you will sense his vileness and recognize that he is an enemy."

"Why do you think the Lord doesn't want us to go to Asia or Bithynia?" Silas asked.

"I'm not sure. Perhaps he knows I am not ready to engage the people there. He knows full well I do not want a repeat of

---

13. Acts 11:27–28.
14. John 10:1–5.
15. 2 Corinthians 11:14.

what happened in Lystra![16] Remember, God led our forefathers out of Egypt via the wilderness rather than the shorter route by way of the Philistines, because he knew they were not ready for war."[17]

"Well, I must say I am enjoying this beautiful valley and these majestic mountains!" Timothy exclaimed energetically. "I've never been this far from home before."[18]

"What is our next stop, Paul?" Silas asked.

"Troas, I believe," he replied, "but that's still a long way off."

Troas – a prosperous Greek city situated on the Aegean Sea – served as the chief port of north-west Asia Minor. In 301 BC, Lysimachus had named this city Alexandria Troas in memory of Alexander III of Macedon.[19] At one time, Julius Caesar had considered making Troas the capital of the Roman Empire. Paul wasted no time reaching out to several people, and soon the trio were followed by a group of enthusiastic new believers, asking many questions. One of these was a learned man called Luke. He was a physician but also a serious student of history and human nature.[20]

---

16. "The opportunity was better embraced at a maturer stage in his ministry than at this one." Keener, *Acts*, 2331.

17. Exodus 13:17–18.

18. For an explanation of Paul's possible route to Troas see, Schnabel, *Early Christian Mission*, 1144–45, and Keener, *Acts*, 2329–30.

19. Schnabel, *Early Christian Mission*, 1145; Keener, *Acts*, 2335; Wilson, *Biblical Turkey*, 376–81; Bruce, *Acts*, 311.

20. Acts 16:8 records that Paul visited Troas, and Luke might have been one of his converts there because it is from this point that the narrative shifts to "we" (see Acts 16:10). Since Acts 20:6–8 describes what seems to be an established base, with believers meeting regularly on the first day of the week, it seems likely that Paul started a church in Troas. Paul must also have visited Troas again since, in 2 Timothy 4:13, he asks Timothy to bring his cloak and

"We need to pray about something important," Paul said one morning before prayers.

"Yes?" Silas responded. "What are we praying about?"

"It may be that the Holy Spirit is leading us to Macedonia."

"Macedonia?" Timothy asked excitedly. "That means we will have to go by sea! I've never been on a big ship before."

"How do you know he is leading us to Macedonia?" Silas inquired.

"Yes, how do you know, Paul?" Luke chimed in. "Last night you were explaining to me about guidance after I read about how the Spirit drove Jesus into the wilderness in that scroll Silas gave me.[21] You were explaining to us how the Holy Spirit prevented you from going into Asia and Bithynia."

"Yes, and do you remember me saying that the Holy Spirit sometimes speaks to us in dreams?"

"I do."

"Well, last night I had a dream in which a man from Macedonia – or at least I am assuming he was from Macedonia – specifically asked us to come to Macedonia to help them."

"Are followers of the Way guided by dreams?" Luke asked, genuinely interested.[22]

"Not in the same way that other people groups are, my treasured physician," Paul said, smiling. "Having said that, though, let me hasten to add that in the past, God often spoke to our ancestors through dreams or visions.[23] Nevertheless, I want us to pray about this because I must be sure that this is

---

scrolls, including the parchments, that he had left there with Carpus. Keener, *Acts*, 2342. Wilson, *Biblical Turkey*, 378.

21. Mark 1:12.

22. Christians were originally known as followers of "the Way" (Acts 9:2; 19:9, 23; 22:4; 24:14, 22).

23. Genesis 20:3, 6; 28:12–15; 37:5–7; 1 Kings 3:5; Job 33:14–17; Matthew 1:20–21.

God guiding us and not the devil tricking us or, even worse, my own misguided longing to know what we should be doing!"

"I understand," Luke said. "So, how do we do this? Do we all pray together asking God to confirm or contradict your dream? Is that how it works?"

Paul smiled as a cherished memory came flooding back. "When our Lord first called Barnabas and me to do the work we have been doing, all the leaders in the church at Antioch fasted and prayed together to confirm what we thought we had heard him say. It was only once we were all of one accord that they laid hands on us and sent us out with their blessing."[24]

"But I am so excited about going on a sea voyage, Paul!" Timothy chirped. "I'm afraid I may convince myself that you are right just so that I can have this experience!"

"That is why we all pray together, my son," Paul explained. "But remember, God often grants us the desires of our hearts!"[25]

"So, I am assuming we will not be eating today," said Silas, feigning disappointment.

"Well, fasting is useful in helping us to focus," Paul replied.

"Not for me, I'm afraid," Luke said. "I find that my belly rumbles are a major distraction."

"Perhaps something as serious as this will quieten your rumblings, brother," Silas laughed, clapping Luke on the back. "Come, let us seek the Lord!"

"I don't like fasting either," Timothy complained. "I'm already famished."

Paul laughed. "You're always famished, Timothy."

They sailed from Troas and spent the night moored off the coast of the rugged island of Samothrace situated in the

---

24. Acts 13:1–3.
25. Psalm 20:4.

northern Aegean Sea. This island was said to be the home of the Sanctuary of the Great Gods, a place where many pagan religious ceremonies were held.[26] They reached Neapolis late the next day.

"So, was that sea voyage all you had hoped it would be?" Paul asked Timothy as they walked along the road leading to Philippi.

"Oh, Paul!" Timothy beamed. "I've never seen water sparkle like that before. And that glorious clear blue colour . . . it was like the sea was a mirror to the clear azure skies above us! And those big, smooth fish that jumped out of the water and swam in front of our ship as if they wanted to play with us! I'd never imagined such a creature."

"It is so good to see the world through your eyes, young man," Luke said, coming up from behind them. "I'm afraid I often take such beauty for granted."

"I hope I never take anything for granted ever again!" Timothy exclaimed. "May every day be as new and fresh as the one before!"

"Ah, but may history also be every bit as exciting to you as the present and the future," Luke said authoritatively. "Take this area, for example. Centuries ago, the people from the island Thasos . . . remember that island we sailed past this morning?" He turned and pointed to the island just off the coast. "They founded Neapolis. They were shipbuilders, you see, and they needed wood for their ships. But their search for wood took them ever further up the hills until one day, quite by accident, they discovered gold."[27]

"Gold?" Timothy echoed.

---

26. See Keener, *Acts*, 2377–79.

27. Descriptions of Philippi (both here and later) are taken from the following sources: Tsevas, *Greece*, 41–57; Nasrallah, *Archaeology*, Chapter 4; and Mee and Spawforth, *Greece*, 413–19.

"Yes, gold. But that is what got them into trouble!" Luke continued. "When King Philip II found out about the gold, he took the town and renamed it after himself."

"Philippi!"

"Yes, young Timothy, Philippi. But it is also known for a famous battle that took place in the area between Mark Anthony and Octavian's armies and Brutus and Cassius's armies."

"Octavian?" Timothy inquired.

"He was later renamed Augustus after he became Caesar."

"Oh."

"But after the war ended, the land was given to the war veterans, and so it became a Roman colony. But it has never been a large city."[28]

"Why?"

"I suppose because it was always a farming community that lived in the area. There is a good underground water supply and a river where the Jewish women come together to pray on their Sabbath."

"Is there no synagogue, then?"

"No."

"Why?"

"Not enough Jewish men, I'm afraid. There must be ten men to constitute a minyan."[29]

"And speaking about Philippi, there it is," Silas said, pointing ahead.

---

28. Tsevas, 39–41.

29. "Minyan" – a Hebrew word that means "number" – refers to the minimum number of males required to constitute a representative "community of Israel." *Encyclopaedia Britannica Online*, "minyan," 2 February 2018, https://www.britannica.com/topic/minyan.

4

Setting Captives Free

Philippi (Acts 16:11–40)

Paul, Silas, and Timothy arrive in Philippi and meet Lydia, a seller of purple goods, who subsequently becomes a believer and offers them hospitality in her home. The chapter also explores the events that lead to Paul and Silas being beaten and imprisoned and describes their eventual release after an earthquake shakes the prison.

They wandered down the streets of the city, taking in the location of various public buildings and other places they might need to visit during their stay, however long that might be. There was a theatre built on the hillside in front of them. Luke informed them that Greek tragedy and comedy used to be performed at this theatre, but since the Romans had occupied the city, it had been transformed into an arena for gladiators and other such blood sports.

Below the theatre was a level, unpaved area that served as the city square, boasting a large market and an open area for public ceremonies or public trials. Since the streets were laid out in a grid pattern, the newcomers found it easy to find their way around and to remember how to retrace their steps to revisit particular places. Paul was always on the lookout for fellow tentmakers, hoping to be employed so that he could earn their keep.

That Sabbath, the four men went looking for the place of prayer Luke had mentioned earlier.

"The river is not far outside the city," Luke said, pointing in the direction of the western gate. "It is easy walking distance from the centre of the city."[1]

"But is it appropriate for us to speak to a group of women, Paul?" Silas asked, sounding concerned.

"I don't see why not," Paul answered. "We are four men, and I am sure they are a fair-sized group. Besides, Jesus taught a group of women, remember? Not to mention that he praised Mary for adopting the posture of a disciple, sitting and learning at his feet."[2]

"Nevertheless, we must be careful," said Luke. "We do not wish to set tongues wagging if we can help it."

"I must say," interrupted Timothy, feeling rather uncomfortable with the present conversation, "this is a very beautiful place. I've never seen so many rose bushes."

"Yes," said Luke enthusiastically, picking up the conversation thread, "they say the roses here have a hundred petals."

"A hundred!"

"Yes, and I for one am glad we are here in autumn to witness their beauty, even if it is at the end of the season. Sadly, we are

---

1. For a detailed discussion on the three possible locations of this river, see Keener, *Acts*, 2386–88.

2. Luke 8:1–3 and Luke 10:38–42. It is interesting that both these references are only found in the Gospel of Luke.

too late for the wildflowers . . . the poppies, daisies, and irises. They blanket the fields with wild splashes of colour in the spring and early summer!"[3]

"I think we have found our place of prayer," Paul said, pointing at a group of women and several young children standing on the grassy embankment of a small river. "Greetings," he called out.

The women turned to look at the new arrivals.

"You are here for prayer?" one of the women asked.

"Yes," Paul replied, "and to bring greetings from Jerusalem, Antioch, and elsewhere."

"Jerusalem? Were you a resident there?" a well-dressed woman asked, stepping forward.

"Yes. I was born and raised in Tarsus in Cilicia, but I went to Jerusalem at a young age to study under the tutelage of Rabbi Gamaliel. Perhaps you have heard of him?"

"Heard of him? Who has not heard of the great teacher?" she replied, obviously impressed.

"Do you perhaps have a word to share?" another woman asked expectantly.

"We do," Paul said, finding a comfortable place to sit.

After exchanging pleasantries, explaining their presence in Philippi, and reciting the first half of the daily prayers, Paul delivered to this little group of women the message of salvation by faith in the death and resurrection of Jesus. While all the women listened with great interest, one in particular seemed completely captivated by what Paul had to say. The men discovered during the ensuing conversation that she was a God-fearer from the city of Thyatira in Asia, a trader of

---

3. Ivana Muratovska, "A Little Something About North Macedonia's Vegetation," *Balkanea*, https://balkanea.com/a-little-something-about-north-macedonia-s-vegetation.

purple goods by occupation, and that her name was Lydia. Paul questioned her for some time about what she believed and was convinced that she had understood the message clearly. Then, after speaking with some children and a few women, Lydia returned and indicated that she and her household wished to be baptized.

"Your household?" Paul asked.

"Yes," Lydia replied, "my four sons and the women who work with me."[4]

"So, you are married?" Luke asked, wondering where her husband might be and how he would respond to her newfound faith.

"In a manner of speaking," she replied, at first looking down as if embarrassed but then quickly lifting her head to look them straight in their eyes, her lips tightly pressed together.

"I beg your pardon." Luke sounded flustered. "I do not mean to pry."

"You have said nothing I have not heard before. The truth is that my husband lives in Thyatira. I live here as his trade agent with our sons."[5]

"And he supplies you with the purple goods you sell?"

"Yes," she said, smiling slightly. "He is my supplier. We use two different dyes in the making of our goods. One is made from shellfish – this is the most expensive and usually bought only by the very wealthy here.[6] The other is made from the root

---

[4]. It is possible that Euodia and Syntyche (see Philippians 4:2) were part of Lydia's faith circle, either as tradeswomen themselves or as Lydia's employees.

[5]. For an in-depth discussion about Lydia's status – especially in view of the fact that the four men stayed in her house without attracting a negative response from the Philippian community – and her trade in purple, see Keener, *Acts*, 2393–408.

[6]. Wikipedia, "Murex," last revised 11 April 2024, https://en.wikipedia.org/w/index.php?title=Murex&oldid=1218404834.

of the madder plant[7] and is less expensive, but it is still a good source of income for me and my sons, especially since we have no competitor in Philippi."

She turned to Paul and asked earnestly, "Is my marital situation a problem?"

"Not in this case, no," Paul replied. "You cannot be held responsible for the actions of another, even if he happens to be your spouse."[8]

"He is not a bad person, you know," she said kindly. "He does provide well for us, but he has his own way of living, if you understand my meaning."

"What is important to me is whether you believe in the Lord Jesus Christ."

"I do," she stated firmly. "You may question my sons and the rest of my household to make sure they believe as I do."

Lydia called her sons, the two women who worked with her, and several servants. One by one, Paul questioned them and then baptized them all in the name of Jesus.

"Where did you find lodging?" Lydia asked, as they began to walk back to the city.

"Well, we have been . . ." Paul began, but Lydia interrupted.

"I do hope that if you consider me faithful, I might prevail on you to lodge in my house?"

"That is most kind, but will we not be a burden to you and your children."

"My mother has a large house, sir," Lydia's eldest son said, in a voice that had not yet broken, "and she has adequate funds."

---

7. Wikipedia, "Rubia tinctorum," last revised 24 May 2024, https://en.wikipedia.org/w/index.php?title=Rubia_tinctorum&oldid=1225490819.

8. See 1 Corinthians 7:12–16 for Paul's advice to Corinthian Christians who were married to unbelievers.

Lydia blushed. "Hush, child, we must not boast." Turning to Paul, she said, "But it is true that my house is large, and you will not inconvenience us at all. Besides, my courtyard could serve as a place of instruction for others, should they, too, come to believe in Jesus."

As Paul was about to speak, she added, "You may sleep in the rooms next to where we keep our goods. That is on the opposite side of the house from where we reside."

"Woman," Paul smiled, "you are very wise and very persuasive. You will make a good evangelist. Thank you, we will accept your gracious hospitality."[9]

Lydia's home became a good place for new believers to meet regularly for prayer and instruction in the Way. But they also continued to meet at the river to reach out to those who gathered there every Sabbath. However, after some days, a young slave girl who was possessed by an evil spirit connected to the Pythian oracle at Delphi – a spirit that gave her the ability to divine and foretell – began to follow Paul and Silas, loudly proclaiming that they were "servants of the Most High God"[10] and revealing that their purpose in Philippi was to preach a message of salvation.[11] This revelation was unwelcome as it attracted the attention of all who heard her. Eventually, after trying his best to ignore her disturbing presence, Paul turned

---

9. On hospitality, see Keener, *Acts*, 2414–20.

10. Although El Elyon (here: *tou theou tou hupsistou* and LXX: *ho theos ho hupsistos*) is used 28 times in reference to God in the Old Testament, it is possible that such a title used in a pagan setting would have been understood as the supreme god over many other gods.

11. The definite article is missing from her statement and thus her message was misleading as it claimed that what Paul and Silas were teaching was merely one way of salvation rather than the only way.

and rebuked the spirit and commanded it to leave the girl which it did at once.

But her sudden loss of mantic abilities meant that her owners could no longer gain from her gifts. They were furious and brought Paul and Silas before the city officials, capitalizing on the general anti-Jewish sentiment at the time and falsely accusing them of propagating customs prohibited for Romans and thus disturbing the peace. This was an effective move on the part of the accusers as Emperor Claudius's expulsion of the Jews from Rome on account of disagreements between those who believed in Jesus and those who did not was well known in all the Roman colonies.[12] The response was swift and vicious. Before Paul or Silas could say a word in self-defence, they had been stripped, brutally beaten, and thrown in the innermost cell of the prison. The jailer had cruelly fastened their feet in the stocks, obviously under the impression that they were men of the lowest social status.[13]

"You know," Paul spoke into the darkness, "every time I suffer for the Way, I think of the many believers I had tortured and beaten when I was as yet an unbeliever."

Silas was breathing hard, the wood of the stocks, the distance between their feet a little too far apart for comfort, and the rough edges of the wall all aggravated the pain he felt from his injuries. "I might not feel so poorly if they had just allowed us to wash and dress our wounds and had given us

---

12. Suetonius mentions that the expulsion of the Jews from Rome was due to persistent difficulties between followers of Christ and unbelieving Jews. Suetonius, *Claud.* 25, and Suetonius, *Tib.* 36 (https://www.perseus.tufts.edu/hopper/text?doc=Perseus:abo:phi,1348,015:25#note5 and https://www.perseus.tufts.edu/hopper/text?doc=Perseus%3Atext%3A1999.02.0132%3Alife%3Dtib.%3Achapter%3D36).

13. See Keener, *Acts*, 2486–88.

back our clothing. I have nothing with which to cover myself. I feel humiliated."

"Public beatings are meant to be humiliating. They are intended to bring as much shame as possible on the accused."

"Stripped and beaten in public like that. I'm embarrassed to admit it, but I soiled myself at some point . . . and to add insult to injury, they just shouted at me and laughed and beat me all the harder."

"I felt nothing but anger and hatred when I persecuted the brethren. I suppose these men feel the same. Nothing but contempt."

"Why didn't you tell them we are Roman citizens? Silas groaned, vigorously rubbing his legs as intense spasms caused them to shake uncontrollably. "They would not have beaten us then – at least not without a proper trial! And the charge against us was false!"

"It all happened so quickly. I did try to speak, but the next thing I knew they were beating every part of my naked body with those rods."

"You know," Silas replied in between gasps, "as they were beating me, I remembered that they stripped our Lord naked, and they beat him, too. At least we were not whipped as he was. We would have much less flesh on our bodies then."

"Ah, yes. Always a reason to rejoice, isn't there? What does Isaiah say? 'He was pierced for our offences and beaten for our sins . . . it is because of his scourging that we are healed.'"[14]

At first, Silas said nothing, trying to take in the gravity of those comforting words. Then he began to sing shakily. "Blessed are you, Lord our God, King of the universe . . ."

Soon their hymns and prayers of praise filled the prison, and the sound flooded out into the night. The prisoners listened

---

14. Isaiah 53:5.

and marvelled as they heard the good news about Jesus in word and song from men who had every reason to be bitter over their harsh ill-treatment. They were astounded by Paul and Silas's firm conviction that their God was with his followers even through trial and suffering.

Suddenly their praise was interrupted by a deep rumbling sound, followed by a terrifying shaking of the ground beneath them. The stones in the walls were dislodged and began to fall around them. The prison doors fell free from their hinges. People outside as well as the other prisoners inside began shrieking in fear. Paul and Silas felt the stocks mercifully loosen from around their ankles, and they quickly stood up and ran to stand in the open doorway for protection.

"Do not flee," Paul shouted to the other loosed prisoners. "Do not flee! Come daylight they will hunt you down and surely put you to death! Stay and wait for your release."

"By all the gods," the jailer shouted to the terrified and immobilized guards as he came running out of his quarters, "what is happening?"

The jailer saw only Paul and Silas standing in the doorway and assumed that the rest of the prisoners had escaped. Paul saw him draw his sword and thought, at first, that the man meant to execute them. Then he saw the jailer turn the sword on himself.[15]

"Stop!" Paul yelled. "Stop! We are all present and accounted for."

---

15. There are two plausible explanations for the attempted suicide. One is that the jailer feared that the authorities might accuse him of negligence and punish or execute him. Judging from the travesty of Paul and Silas's "trial," the Philippian authorities do not appear to have been reasonable or fair. The other possibility is that the suicide was to avoid disgrace. Keener, *Acts*, 2498–507.

"What?" the jailer could hardly believe his ears. He dropped his sword. "You there," he shouted at a frozen guard, "move and find a light!"

The other guards suddenly overcame their fear and rushed in, brandishing lanterns and torches.

"*You* two!" the jailer said to Paul and Silas when he saw their faces in the torchlight. "The mantic declared that you were servants of the Most High God. She said you proclaimed the way of salvation. Did your God do this? Or are you yourselves gods?"

Before Paul could say anything, the man fell before them, trembling greatly and weeping from fear. When he had regained his composure, he brought them out, leaving the guards to secure the other prisoners.

"Tell me, please," he begged, "what is this message of salvation? What must I do to be saved?"

"Believe in the Lord Jesus," Paul said.

"If you believe in him, you will be saved," Silas added. "You and your household."

"Jesus? Who is Jesus?" And then, suddenly realizing that Paul and Silas stood naked and wounded before him, he added, "Forgive me. Allow me to escort you to my quarters. You can tell us more while I wash and clean your wounds."

"May we please cover our nakedness before we expose ourselves to your family?" Silas implored.

"Oh, forgive me. What must you think of me?" said the jailer. "You there!" he called to another guard. "Bring the prisoners' clothes."

As they waited, Paul continued to explain to the jailer the good news of salvation through Jesus. As in the case of Lydia, the Lord opened his mind to understand – as well as the members of his family who subsequently joined him – and they all believed.

There was a well of water close by, on one side of the prison, and after the jailer washed the dirt and the dried blood from their backs and legs, dressing each open wound and welt, Paul poured water on each individual, baptizing them in the name of the Father and of the Son and of the Holy Spirit. It was a mutual washing that brought both physical and spiritual healing.

After they had eaten with the rejoicing family, Paul and Silas lay down on some warm straw and slept.

When morning came, the jailer brought the news that the city officials had sent a message saying that they were free to leave.

Paul yawned and rubbed the sleep out of his eyes. "No," he said simply.

"Excuse me?" The jailer was surprised.

"No!" Paul repeated insistently. "They beat us publicly without a proper trial."

"Yes?" The jailer urged him to continue.

"We are Roman citizens."[16]

"What?" he gasped. "Both of you?"

"Yes," Silas groaned as he carefully rose to a sitting position. "We are both Roman citizens. Your officials humiliated us and imprisoned us, and now they want us to leave without a word. Do you think that is right?"

"I will not leave unless they come personally to release us," Paul said flatly.

"You do realize that you can be severely punished or even executed for making false citizenship claims?"[17]

---

16. Beating and imprisoning Roman citizens without a proper trial was a criminal offence.

17. Falsely claiming to be a Roman citizen was equally serious a crime and could result in execution (Suetonius, *Claud*. 25.3 – https://www.perseus.tufts.edu/hopper/text?doc=Perseus:abo:phi,1348,015:25).

"Our claims are not false. Besides, it is for your own sake, as well as for the sake of the other new believers in Philippi that I am raising this issue now. In the future, they will think twice before mistreating anyone who proclaims our message."

"I understand. But what if they do not believe you?"

"Seriously, think about it. Would a released prisoner bring up such a subject? Would they not simply be thankful for their freedom and leave? No, my dear brother, they will not wish to prolong their own embarrassment by challenging my claim."

"Very well, I will send your message to the officials."

It was not long before the officials arrived, apologizing fervently but also pleading with Paul and Silas to leave the city. It was obvious that they wanted to minimize the self-inflicted damage done to their own reputations.

"We will depart," Paul said slowly and firmly, "once we have had sufficient time to take appropriate leave of our brethren here."

"Certainly, certainly," one of the officials whined, rubbing his hands together as if washing them in mid-air. "But I do believe it is best for all concerned if you both leave as soon as possible. The owners of the girl, you see . . ." It seemed clear the officials did not wish to lose face before their constituents and Paul and Silas' continued presence in the city would make people question the initial trial, sentencing, and punishment.

The jailer and his family walked with them to Lydia's home so that Paul and Silas could introduce themselves to the other believers. Timothy wept unashamedly when Paul and Silas walked through the door. It was a merry reunion, especially since Lydia informed them that she had purchased the young slave girl from her previous owners and brought her home to raise as her own daughter.[18]

---

18. This is fictional but possible.

"Paul," Luke said, as he walked with Paul to the gate of the city, "I have decided to stay here."

"You have?"

"Yes, for two reasons. For one, I can serve as a teacher of the Way to new converts."

"That would be wonderful. Thank you, Luke."

"Yes, well, the second reason is . . ."

"You want to finish copying out those notes of Mark's, don't you?" Paul asked, smiling.

"I do. But I would also like to begin compiling my own work, using his notes as well as my own research."

"That, my dear brother, is an excellent notion."

The two men were about to hug when Paul gingerly stepped away from the embrace.

"Forgive me, I am still far too tender. Perhaps next time, Luke."

"Yes. Next time."

5

Painful Gains – Power and Pain

Thessalonica (Acts 17:1–9)

> Paul, Silas, and Timothy travel to Thessalonica and preach in the synagogue, resulting in many Jews and Greeks becoming believers. They face from the unbelieving Jews, who form a mob and attack the home of Jason, where Paul and his companions are staying. This leads to Paul and Silas being forced to leave the city.

It had taken them six days to get to Thessalonica via Amphipolis and Apollonia.[1] Paul and Silas were still recovering from their wounds, and they had to make frequent stops to make sure the wounds were clean and not festering, applying fresh herbs and clean bandages regularly. As they did not wish to reopen scars or aggravate bruises, Timothy carried most of their small

---

1. Weima, *1–2 Thessalonians*, 24–25.

amount of baggage. Thankfully, the large lakes along the way supplied them with ample fresh water to drink and fresh fish to eat.

Thessalonica was a bustling port city and an important commercial centre. Strategically located on the Via Egnatia – the major trade route connecting Rome to the east – the city served as the capital of the Roman province of Macedonia. Its population was mixed, consisting of Romans, Greeks, and Jews, as well as other ethnic groups. The city was well known, not only for its thriving economy but also for its cultural and religious diversity, with numerous temples dedicated to Greek, Roman, and Egyptian gods.

Compared with Philippi, the city centre was huge and impressive, luxuriously paved with marble, and the portico that surrounded it was covered with a roof supported by large columns. Paul found a group of Jewish tentmakers and asked if they might need a helping hand.[2] As all three men were ethnic Jews, these tentmakers were willing to let them stay in the back of the building until they could find more suitable lodgings – possibly with the owner of the shop, a man by the name of Jason.[3] Through this group of tentmakers, Paul and his companions learned that there was a substantial Jewish community in the city, and so they made plans to go there on the Sabbath.

"That was quite a message you brought us today, Paul," Jason said as they stepped out of the synagogue. "I'd like to hear more, so if you and your companions are willing, please accept my offer of hospitality."

"That is very generous of you, thank you," Paul replied.

---

2. 1 Thessalonians 2:9.
3. See Acts 17:5, 7.

"Not generous so much as selfish, I think," Jason said, laughing. "I want to benefit from your teaching as much as I can."

After three consecutive Sabbaths, a significant number of Jews, including Aristarchus[4] – one of Paul's fellow tentmakers – and several God-fearers and leading women of the city had come to trust in Jesus, and Jason's house soon became the centre for this growing community of believers. While Paul taught the group in the evenings, he continued to share the gospel with his gentile customers and others in the marketplace by day, and, to his great joy, many of them abandoned their former idol worship to put their faith in Jesus. The Holy Spirit was turning the hearts of many.[5]

Following the example of Jesus,[6] Paul began teaching them from the Torah, then moving on to the Writings and the Prophets, showing them from the Scriptures that the cross, far from being foolishness or a cause for stumbling, was central to all that had been written before.[7] He exhorted them to live lives worthy of their calling, warning them that Jesus would return one day to judge the living and the dead.[8] His arrival would come as a surprise to many just as in the days of Noah when – before the flood – people went about their day-to-day lives without any impending sense of doom.[9]

On more than one occasion, the Philippians graciously sent financial aid,[10] making it possible for Paul to spend less time

---

4. Acts 20:4.
5. 1 Thessalonians 1:4–5.
6. Luke 24:27, 44–48.
7. 1 Corinthians 1:22–24.
8. 2 Timothy 4:1.
9. Matthew 24:37–39.
10. Philippians 4:15–16.

making tents and more time persuading both the unbelieving Jews and the Gentiles. Together with Silas and Timothy, he also instructed the new believers on how to live in a manner worthy of God[11] and trained future leaders for the new community.[12]

Unfortunately, many of the idle social elite misunderstood Paul's shift in strategy and thought that they, too, were exempt from working for a living. Paul admonished them, urging the believers to be wary of such behaviour and pointing out that he paid for food with money he had earned from his labours. "Those who refuse to work," he said, "should not scrounge off others."[13]

But what amazed Paul was the speed at which most of these new believers began to spread the word themselves. Soon many people, even in the surrounding areas, were talking about the faith of these Thessalonian brethren.[14]

Sadly, Paul's success in winning so many converts to Jesus from among both the Jewish and gentile populations soon attracted a negative response from the now dwindling Jewish community. They rounded up several malingerers and layabouts from the marketplace to form an unruly mob who caused an uproar in the city and attacked Jason's house in their search for Paul and Silas. Not finding these men there, they grabbed Jason and a few of the new believers instead and dragged them before the city authorities.

The nature of the charges brought against Paul and Silas suggested that their accusers were relying, for their case, on common knowledge about the recent expulsion of Jews from Rome because of persistent antagonism between followers of

---

11. 1 Thessalonians 2:12.

12. 1 Thessalonians 5:12–13.

13. 2 Thessalonians 3:6–11.

14. 1 Thessalonians 1:8.

Jesus and the unbelieving Jews.[15] This expulsion dovetailed nicely into the next charge which was Paul and Silas's apparent flagrant disregard for an imperial edict against any form of prediction of a future or alternative king.[16] These charges were indeed serious because if the city was seen to be a haven for insurrectionists, it stood to lose its preferential position as a favoured city in the Roman Empire. Given that the city had regained administrative privileges lost under the reign of Tiberius only six years earlier, this fear was real.

But unlike the officials in Philippi, these authorities seemed to have seen through the deceptive ploy and did not give in to the demands of the crowd. However, they did take a security deposit from Jason with the understanding that there would be no more disturbances. The implication was clear. Paul and Silas were henceforth banned from the city.[17]

---

15. Suetonius mentions that the expulsion of the Jews from Rome was due to persistent difficulties between followers of Christ and unbelieving Jews, Suetonius, *Claud.* 25, and Suetonius, *Tib.* 36, https://www.perseus.tufts.edu/hopper/text?doc=Perseus:abo:phi,1348,015:25#note5 and https://www.perseus.tufts.edu/hopper/text?doc=Perseus%3Atext%3A1999.02.0132%3Alife%3Dtib.%3Achapter%3D36.

16. Weima, *1-2 Thessalonians*, 33–34.

17. 1 Thessalonians 2:18.

6

Persecutors and Philosophers

Berea and Athens (Acts 17:10–15; 16–34)

> Paul, Silas, and Timothy travel to Berea and preach in the synagogue, leading to many Jews and Greeks becoming believers. Once again they face opposition from the Thessalonian Jews, who follow them to Berea and stir up trouble. This results in Paul being escorted by the Berean believers to Athens, where he preaches in both the synagogue and the marketplace, interacting with the Athenians and their philosophies, and, eventually, addresses the Areopagus.

"But why Berea of all places?" Paul complained, as they walked swiftly on, after having left Thessalonica under cover of darkness. "We could have simply continued on the road to the coast and then taken a ship to Rome."[1]

"Jason said it was a town considered out of the way,"[2] Silas replied, slightly out of breath, "that would be a haven for us until things calm down in Thessalonica. If anyone should attempt to follow us, it's more likely that they would expect us to go west or south on the main roads, not along the minor ones."

"Besides, he has contacts there, so we won't have to look for a place to stay," Timothy added, ever the practical one.

"All true," said Paul. With a spark of hope in his voice, he added, "And best of all is that if things do calm down in Thessalonica, Berea is not far if we are allowed to return."

"Rome was not really an option, though, was it?" Silas asked. "Didn't they say that the Emperor had expelled all Jews from the city?"

"Yes," Paul sighed. "It seems that many of my hopes and plans have been hindered or prevented on this trip. Nevertheless, I do believe that it is the Lord who leads and guides our footsteps, and so I am content."

"The author of Proverbs tells us to trust God completely and not rely on our own limited reasoning," Timothy said. "If we consistently consult him in faithful prayer, he will guide our ways."[3]

"A good word," affirmed Silas, "and a great encouragement."

"My only concern," said Paul, as they turned off the Via Egnatia onto the road towards Berea, "is that someone will say that to escape prosecution and persecution, I abandoned the

---

1. It is possible that Paul's statement that he had often planned to visit Rome (Romans 1:13) is a reference to this diversion among others.

2. Cicero, *Pis.* 89, https://www.loebclassics.com/view/marcus_tullius_cicero-in_pisonem/1931/pb_LCL252.139.xml.

3. Proverbs 3:5–6.

flock . . . or that I am guilty and that's why I fled . . . or, even worse, that I am only interested in what I can get out of other people – like their praise or their money. They may say that I used these people for my own gain."[4]

"Everyone knows that none of that is true, Paul," Silas rasped, still out of breath because of the fast pace at which they were walking. "We left for the protection of Jason and the others."

"But we left them, Silas. We left them, and there is still so much they need to learn!"

"Well, I can return if you like," Timothy offered. "No one except our brethren knows who I am."

Paul stopped, turned, and placed his hands on Timothy's shoulders. "You are more than a beloved son to me, Timothy. I don't want to place you in harm's way."[5]

"And you are a father to me. For this, I will always be grateful. But surely, in your wisdom, you can see that no one will think a young man like me can be any threat to the establishment. Everyone says that I have a baby face and look much younger than I am. Most folks don't take much notice of me because of my apparent youthfulness."[6]

"What you lack in years, you make up for in your godly behaviour!" said Silas encouragingly.

Paul sighed. "The sun will rise in a few hours. We need to find a place to rest for whatever is left of this night. My head will be clearer after a good sleep."

---

4. 1 Thessalonians 2:1–16.
5. Philippians 2:20, 22.
6. 1 Timothy 4:12.

"We are intrigued with your message, Paul," Sopater said enthusiastically.[7] "We have a few scrolls here that we read from and discuss at our house of study, and we would be grateful if you would take us through them to show how what you say is true."

"I would be honoured," Paul replied. "When do you meet?"

"Every day before and after work."

"Every day?"

"Yes."

"That is extraordinary."

"Yes," Sopater laughed, "so our brothers in Thessalonica tell us. But we are serious men, and as pilgrims in a foreign land, we believe we must be careful not to lose touch with what is true. Many of our younger kinsfolk have embraced gentile ways."

"Am I right in assuming that you have many God-fearers here as well?"

"Yes, and several noble Greek women and men who are seekers."

"Well, we could take three different groups and work through the scrolls with them."

"Three?"

"Yes, one each for Silas, Timothy, and me."

"Timothy? Does such a young man know enough of the Scriptures to teach the more senior and learned among us?"

"He looks much younger than he is. But do not despise his youth.[8] He knows the Scriptures better than many twice his age."[9]

---

7. It is possible that the Sopater, son of Pyrrhus, who is mentioned in Acts 20:4, was converted during this period.

8. 1 Timothy 4:12.

9. 2 Timothy 3:14–15; see also, 2 Timothy 1:5.

"Then I wish to be part of his group. This is something worth seeing!"

It was not long before word of the conversion of many Jews and Gentiles in Berea reached the ears of the unbelieving Jews in Thessalonica. A delegation was immediately dispatched to alarm and confuse the uninformed crowds with the same lies they had used effectively before.

"It would be better for you and all of us if you left Macedonia altogether," said Sopater, hastily packing a bag of provisions for Paul. "If you remain in this province, they will not stop harassing you."

"But where will he go?" Timothy asked, concerned for his beloved mentor's safety.

"Achaia . . . go to Athens, Paul. We will go with you to the coast and take you there by ship. There is safety in numbers, and one can appear invisible in a group."

"Very well," Paul acceded, "I will let your wisdom guide me."

"It is such a tragedy," Sopater said sadly. "We were learning so much, especially from young Timothy here."

"We don't have to go with you, Paul, do we?" Silas ventured. "We can stay and teach. It is you they want to silence."

"That is true," Timothy added. "Besides, as I said before, I am in no danger. People don't take notice of me because they think I am too young to know anything useful."

"Ah, if they only knew!" Sopater beamed. "You may be the most persuasive one of all! It is good for our youth to be instructed by one so young himself. But come, we must go quickly. We do not want to give them enough time to even begin to formulate a charge against you, Paul."

The three men hugged and prayed for each other before Paul and a group of new Berean believers disappeared into the night.

"Tell Silas and Timothy to come and meet me here in Athens as soon as possible," said Paul, hugging his newfound friends goodbye as they stood on the harbour walls. "And thank you for bringing me here safely."

"You are welcome, Paul," Sopater said, holding Paul tightly against his chest. "You have given us the greatest gift a man can give. You have given us freedom . . . you have given us life."

"Promise me you will continue the work when you return."

"I am sure we can work together with our brothers in Thessalonica to ensure that the faith goes out everywhere! How can we not share such good news? It would be an offence to God not to tell others about Jesus!"

"Farewell, my brother. Go with God!"

"And God go with you!"

The city of Athens was a large and bustling port city with three harbours. It was surrounded by mountains to the north, west, and south, and Paul counted no less than seven hills dominating the city itself. Although he had been told that Athens now enjoyed diminished political power – having been surpassed by both Corinth and Ephesus – the city was still considered the centre of Greek culture, boasting no less than four philosophical schools.[10] While he waited for Silas and Timothy to arrive, Paul acquainted himself with the layout of the city, ever on the lookout for fellow tentmakers.

---

10. Schnabel, *Early Christian Mission*, 1171.

But as he walked, Paul was astounded by the sheer number of sanctuaries and temples and the abundance of idols displayed everywhere in the streets. To be sure, there had been many along the way as he walked from the harbour into the city, but nothing could have prepared him for the overabundance of images and figures within the confines of the city itself. "How is it possible to have so many gods?" he wondered. "What fear drives a person to create gods for every possible event or misfortune in life? Did they ever think they had perhaps missed one?" Rounding a corner, he saw the answer to his question. There stood an empty altar with this inscription: "To an Unknown God."

Paul knew that Jews had inhabited this city for centuries. Had they done nothing to counter this wholesale pagan environment? Had their monotheistic faith and practice had no impact at all? Had they compromised their faith? Or had they simply kept their faith to themselves, having no positive effect on the myriads of cultures represented in such a multi-ethnic city?

It was not hard to find the synagogue, and Paul entered it to reason with the Jews and devout persons who gathered there. Later, in the city centre, he engaged daily in debates with anyone who would listen, both Jews and Greeks alike.

Some Epicurean and Stoic philosophers[11] who heard him speak also engaged him in conversation. For the most part, the Epicureans considered Paul an idle chatterer because he did not employ the typical cultured style of the Athenians, who wrote out oratories appropriate to the circumstances and to their hearers. But the Stoics were fascinated with what they wrongly assumed to be his doctrine of two foreign gods, namely, Jesus

---

11. For a detailed study on Epicureans and Stoics, see Keener, *Acts*, 2584–95.

and the Anastasis – that is, the Resurrection. Impressed and curious about his teachings, they invited him to the Areopagus.

"May we know what this new teaching is that you are presenting?" they asked sincerely. "For you bring some strange things to our ears. We wish to know, therefore, what these things mean."

One man added, "We Athenians and many foreigners who live here love to hear and debate new ideas."

Standing before the esteemed council of philosophers, Paul prayed a quick silent prayer for wisdom and for the right words to say.[12] He was so grateful that his father had made him study the Greek poets and philosophers as several texts came to mind as he was formulating his argument in his head.[13]

"Men of Athens," Paul began, in an authoritative voice, "as I walked about your city, I noticed that you are very devout, with many altars and statues dedicated to various gods. While I was wandering around, I even stumbled upon an altar with the inscription 'To an Unknown God,' and this made me wonder whether you realized that you are worshipping a God you do not yet fully know."

Paul looked at his audience and saw that they were all leaning forward, brimming with anticipation.

"Allow me, if I may, to introduce you to this God whom you do not yet know. My God is the creator of the world and everything in it. Unlike the gods made of gold or stone, this God doesn't need our service as he owns everything. Indeed, everything exists and continues to exist because he wills it so. This God does not need temples or buildings made by human hands. He is not far from any of us; in fact, we live and move and exist because of him."

---

12. Luke 12:11–12.

13. See van der Bijl, *Galatians*, 4–5.

Paul swallowed hard. His mouth felt as dry as dust.

"You see," he continued, "from one person, he made every nation on earth, and he has arranged things so that we might seek him and find him, though he's not far from any of us. He alone determined their times and the places where they would live. Because of this, people might have worshipped this God instinctively in the past, but now he is calling everyone to turn away from ignorance and embrace the truth. He is patient, giving everyone time to rethink their ways."

Paul noticed a few frowns on the faces of some of the men.

"Dear God," he prayed silently, "help me to quote from their own writers so that they might understand."

"You see, this God is not some distant deity. On the contrary, he is intimately involved in each of our lives, giving us everything we need, even the very breath in our lungs. As some of your own poets have written, 'In him we live and move and exist[14] because we are his creatures.'"[15]

He noticed some approving nods and heard affirmative murmurs. With growing eloquence and conviction, Paul pressed on.

"As God is the sovereign creator of all life, you cannot possibly believe that he can be represented in the likes of gold, silver, or stone images. No human being, regardless of their expertise or skill, can fashion something that would adequately embody his likeness. In the past, God disregarded your misguided worship as he knew you were ignorant of the truth, but now, because I have made him known to you, he is expecting everyone to turn away from their old ways and embrace this new understanding. Why? Because this God has fixed a day on which he will judge the world in righteousness

---

14. Epimenides, *Cretica*.
15. Aratus, *Phaen*.

through a man whom he has ordained, giving us assurance of this by raising this man from the dead."

At this point, when they heard Paul mention the resurrection from the dead, some scoffed, but others wanted to hear more.

"We want to hear more about this, Paul," several said. Among them was Dionysius – a member of the Areopagus – and a woman named Damaris, along with several others who believed. These people believed Paul's message and followed him.

In the heart of Greek intellectual and cultural thought, the message of Jesus met with both opposition and acceptance. Nevertheless, the seeds of faith had been sown, and Paul began to teach the new believers. Having been reunited with Paul in Athens, Silas and Timothy also assisted him for a short period, but since Paul was anxious about the well-being of the believers in Macedonia, he sent Silas to Philippi[16] and Timothy to Thessalonica,[17] after having instructed them to meet him later in Corinth.

---

16. Schnabel, *Early Christian Mission*, 1169.
17. 1 Thessalonians 3:1–5.

7

Encouragement and Exhortation

Corinth (Acts 18:1–11; 1 Thessalonians 1:1–2:16)

> Paul writes his first letter to the Thessalonians. The group prays for guidance, and Paul outlines the structure of the letter. He emphasizes his genuine care for the Thessalonians, defends himself against accusations, and encourages righteous living in anticipation of Christ's return.

"Paul?" Timothy's voice seemed to be echoing from a distant place. "Paul, are you listening?"

"What?" Paul replied, slowly emerging from his review of his travels since leaving Jerusalem.

"Our brethren are leaving. Some would like to greet you before they go."

Paul groaned as he stood up. His body was aching. Priscilla was right. He needed to rest more.

"If you still want to write that letter," Silas said, "now would be a good time . . . but if you're too tired, it can wait."

"No," Paul said, dismissively, "it must be written sooner rather than later."

"Aquila has given me all the writing materials we need, but it may be best if we go down to the workshop so that Priscilla and Aquila can get some sleep."

"Nonsense," said Priscilla, overhearing them. "Who will keep you supplied with refreshments as you write?"

"As ever the gracious hostess," Paul laughed. "Thank you. But let me greet our brethren first, then we can start. It shouldn't take long. I have most of what I want to say in my head already."

"And I will begin to prepare some nourishment for us all."

"Shall I be your scribe?" Silas asked, after the group had spent a long time praying, asking the Holy Spirit to guide them in the writing of the letter.

"If you wouldn't mind," Paul replied, "that would be a tremendous help."

"Would you mind terribly if I looked over your shoulder as you write, Silas?" Timothy asked. "I think you can teach me a lot."

"Why would I mind?" asked Silas, smiling. "Next time, you can be the scribe! Besides, you can help sharpen the quills when they get blunt and be the keeper of the parchment."

"I want to write this letter in five parts," Paul said, as he sat with his back to the outside wall. "When I wrote the letter to the Galatians, I was so distressed that my letter lacked a good structure."

"I am ready, but please do speak slowly and clearly. I don't want to get anything wrong."

"Stop me whenever you like."

Paul sat and thought for a short while. Then he said, "Paul, Silvanus,[1] and Timothy, to the church[2] of the Thessalonians in God the Father and the Lord Jesus: Grace and peace to you. Do you have that?"

"One moment . . . Grace and peace to you. Yes."

"Now, I want to start with something positive. We can address their concerns later."

"You could begin by giving thanks for them . . . tell them how you always mention them in your daily prayers," Timothy ventured.[3]

---

1. "The longer name was the one commonly known and used in Greek and Roman communities (2 Cor 1:19; 1 Thess 1:1; 2 Thess 1:1; 1 Pet 5:12) whereas the shorter name was employed in Jewish circles (Acts 15:22, 27, 32, 40; 16:19, 25, 29; 17:4, 10, 14, 15; 18:5)." Weima, *1–2 Thessalonians*, 67.

2. "Although the noun *ekklesia* (church) in secular Greek refers to an officially summoned assembly of citizens (see Acts 19:32, 39, 41), in the LXX it (or its verbal cognate) describes the people of God, whether they are assembled for worship or not (see, e.g., Deut 9:10; 18:6; 23:2-4; 31:30; Judg 20:2; 1 Sam 17:47; 1 Chron 28:8; Neh 13:1). In light of the Jewish heritage of Paul, as well as his references to the 'church(es) of God,' both later in this letter (1 Thess 2:14) and elsewhere (e.g., 1 Cor 1:2; 10:32; 11:16; 15:9; 2 Cor 1:1; Gal 1:13), 'it seems unreasonable to doubt that in 1 Thess 1:1 Paul is thinking of the Christians of Thessalonica as members of the 'Church of God,' and that he is fully aware of the biblical background and theological implications of his use of the term' (Deidun 1981: 11; also Malherbe 2000: 99). That the term *ekklesia* reflects Paul's understanding of the predominantly *Gentile* church of Thessalonica as the new people of God is confirmed by his reference to them a mere three verses later as those who are 'loved by God' and who know their 'election' (1:4), terms similarly used in the OT to refer to Israel but now applied to NT believers." Weima, 68.

3. For the sake of this narrative, I am making Silas and Timothy co-authors of – or at least contributors to – the letter. For a contrary position, see Weima, 66.

"Yes," said Silas, "and tell them you remember their works of faith[4] and their labour of love and their patient hope[5] in Jesus."

"Yes, that's good. Reword what you both said as you think best."

Silas thought for a moment and then told them what he was going to write.[6]

"That's good," Paul said, nodding approval.

He waited for Silas to finish writing, then continued, "Now, they need to know that their salvation did not come about by their own volition but because they are loved and chosen by God.[7] They did not just hear our gospel in word only but also in power . . . both in the Holy Spirit and in the boldness of our proclamation as they had first-hand knowledge of how we conducted ourselves while among them."[8]

"Yes," Timothy agreed, "they believed because the Holy Spirit opened their minds and gave them the ability to believe. Just like with Lydia. You didn't trick them into believing."

"Not only that, but I think we set an example for them to follow in that our conduct matched our teaching," Silas added. "It's important for them to remember this if they are to counter the accusations of deception levelled against you, Paul."

---

4. "Works of faith" here refers to works that are the fruit of faith. Paul is not saying that their faith is the result of works but, rather, that their works are the natural outflow of their faith.

5. Or "steadfast" hope. Despite opposition, and perhaps even violent persecution, the Thessalonians' hope in Jesus did not waver.

6. Since writing materials were costly, no scribe would have first written a letter and then sought approval.

7. Deuteronomy 7:7–10.

8. There is no mention of the miraculous in Luke's recording of Paul's ministry among the Thessalonians. For this reason, I understand the "power" to refer to the opening of their hearts to Paul's message, as with Lydia. In my opinion, this power of the Spirit is more miraculous than physical manifestations of power since non-believers are dead in their trespasses and sins and, consequently, must experience spiritual resurrection.

"But what is most important," Paul added, "because it is encouraging for them as well as for us, not to mention good evidence against our detractors, is that they began to imitate us and the Lord. They embraced the word with the joy of the Holy Spirit – even during a time of considerable suffering – to become exemplary models[9] to all who believe in Macedonia and Achaia."

"And still, even today," Timothy added, "despite ongoing suffering, they continue to tell everyone about their newfound faith."

"Yes," Paul said, "I need to encourage them in their exemplary evangelism. Let me think."

Paul lifted his head as if in prayer for a moment and then said, "For from you the word of the Lord echoed outwards[10] not only in Macedonia and Achaia but also in every place your faith towards God is known so that we do not need to say anything about you to anyone else. And, as such, you yourselves declare the manner of our relationship with you – how you turned

---

9. These models are like moulds from which the lives of other believers are cast. So, both Paul and the Lord served as moulds for the Thessalonians. The question does arise as to how Paul and Jesus "received" the word in the context of opposition. It may be that Paul had in mind the choice made by Jesus to follow the Father's instructions despite the very real desire to opt out of the severe suffering that awaited him on the cross. Similarly, Paul did not shrink from obeying what he believed to be God's command even when the consequences led to beatings and imprisonment.

10. The word "echoed" indicates that their evangelism was expanding and reverberating everywhere.

away from idolatry[11] to serve[12] the living and true God,[13] all the while eagerly anticipating the return of his Son, Jesus, from heaven, whom he resurrected from the dead to rescue us from the wrath to come."[14]

"Stop! Stop!" Silas complained. "You are going too fast."

"Come to think of it, it really is no wonder the unbelieving Thessalonians reacted and are reacting so badly," Timothy interjected. "They probably think that the behaviour of our brethren might invoke the anger of the gods from Mount Olympus and that they would be punished collectively if they do not do something to counter what they think of as sacrilege."

"Not to mention the rejection of the imperial cult," Priscilla said, bringing cups of barley water for them to drink. "They may fear that this could lead to their favoured status as a free city being rescinded."

"Thank you, Priscilla," Paul said, taking a cup. "Yes, that's true. The response of the unbelievers is understandable, especially that of the Jews – given what has happened in Rome –

---

11. Modern readers may not understand how this brief statement about their turning away from idols relates to their ongoing suffering. But if one contemplates the reactions of family and friends even today in some religions when one of their members convert to Christianity, one can only imagine the intense feelings of anger levelled at them.

12. The word "doulos" means to "serve as a slave." See Weima, *1–2 Thessalonians*, 109.

13. On the use of "living" God, see Numbers 14:21, 28; Deuteronomy 32:40; Joshua 3:10; Daniel 6:26; for "true," see Exodus 34:6 (LXX); 2 Chronicles 15:3; Psalm 86:15 (LXX); Isaiah 65:16. For the use of both "living" and "true" together, see Jeremiah 10:10. If Paul had in mind these Old Testament texts, then his understanding of their turning away from their previous way of life might be viewed in the same light as the Hebrews leaving Egypt in the exodus event. It was a radical turning away.

14. The mention of their future hope and vindication in terms of "resurrection" and "rescue" is mentioned here in anticipation of what Paul will later say concerning those who had died while awaiting the return of Jesus.

but that does not give them the right to slander me concerning the substance of my intentions and my conduct."

"No," Timothy agreed. "Indeed, it does not."

"So, Silas, in this next section, I want to lay out a defence for what I did while I was with them, and I also want to explain why I have not yet returned to Thessalonica. I do not want them to doubt my integrity nor my love for them."

"I'm ready," Silas said, gulping down the last swallow of barley water.

"Write this," Paul said, eyes closed once more, deep in thought. "As you already know, brethren, our coming to you was not insincere. Through our God, we were bold enough to speak to you about the gospel of God despite much opposition and despite having suffered and been insulted in Philippi, as you are well aware."

"Yes," Timothy agreed, "a trickster would have thought twice about preaching a message that provoked such humiliation and violence!"

"And," Silas added, as he finished writing what Paul had said, "our brethren in Thessalonica did not only hear about this abuse from us but also from the brethren who came bringing gifts from Philippi."[15]

"As you said, they also know that you did not change your message when their fellow citizens opposed you," Timothy said. "Your boldness in delivering your message speaks of an absence of pretence, deceit, or hypocrisy."

Paul did not react to these statements. His eyes were still closed, and he raised one hand as if to write in the air.

Then he went on, "As God has granted us the authority to be entrusted with the gospel, our exhortation was not delivered as trickery, or from an improper motivation, nor with deceit –

---

15. Philippians 4:16.

because we do not speak to please human beings but God, who is the one who examines all hearts."

"I do find it strange," Timothy interrupted, "that your detractors claim you tried to trick our brethren for self-gain. I mean it's not like you were luring them with bait[16] as if you were some travelling illusionist. Or even that you were a self-centred show-off craving approval."

Paul continued as if he had not heard a word. "For neither did we approach you with words of flattery, as you well know, nor with a pretext of covetousness, as God is witness . . ."

He paused, opened his eyes, and then, looking at Timothy with a smile, added, "nor seeking praise from people, neither from you nor from others, even though we could have demanded such respect since we are apostles of Christ. Instead, we were like infants among you."

Paul stopped, rubbed his chin, closed his eyes once more and then continued. "Yes, we were like infants among you. And, like a nursing mother should cherish her children, so, because we cherished you so much, we were well pleased to impart to you not only the gospel of God but also our own souls because you have become beloved to us."

"Wait!" Silas exclaimed. "I can't keep up."

"That's brilliant!" Timothy applauded. "Infants are not capable of deception, nor can they be underhanded in their dealings. They are innocent."

"Yes," Paul said, opening his eyes and smiling. "That's a saying the Jews ought to recognize."

"Oh?" Timothy probed. "Why?"

---

16. The word often translated here as "deceit" "originally referred to catching fish by using bait." Weima, *1–2 Thessalonians*, 135.

"Because it is a statement from Philo. He argued that the greatest liar can't invent a charge against an infant because they are wholly innocent."[17]

"And nursing mothers do not trick their suckling babes either," Priscilla commented. "Mothers only ever want the very best for their children."

"As do fathers," Aquila interjected. "We work hard to provide for our families."

"Indeed, you do," Paul agreed. "And that's a very good image for them, given that I am accused of using our brethren for financial gain. Silas, do you need a break?"

"No, but if you can give me just a moment," Silas said. "I need another quill, please, Timothy. Great, thank you. You can sharpen that one while I use this one. Aquila, would you mind moving that oil lamp a little closer, please? Oh yes, on that stand would be wonderful. Thank you. Alright, go ahead, Paul. I'm ready."

"You're sure you don't want to take a quick break?"

"I'm sure. Go on, please."

"Okay, then write this: 'For you remember brethren that when we proclaimed to you the gospel of God, we laboured and toiled night and day, working so that we might not put a burden on anyone.'"

He paused, waiting for Silas to finish writing.

"Got it."

Paul closed his eyes once more and continued. "Both you and God are witnesses to how devout and righteous and blameless we were among those of you who believed, even as you know how, as a father with his own children, we cared for each one of you, exhorting and urging you and appealing to

---

17. Philo, *Spec. Laws* 3.119, https://www.earlychristianwritings.com/yonge/book29.html.

you to walk in a way that is worthy of the one calling you to his own kingdom and glory."

"Childlike innocence, motherly love, and dependable fatherly devotion," Aquila marvelled. "These metaphors do not just conjure up images of familial ties but also grant you an authoritative role in your dealings with them."[18]

"Well," Timothy added, "I must say that even though I have no first-hand knowledge of my own father caring for me, I do have your example, Paul."

"As do the Thessalonians," Silas added.

"But there's more to this image than care," Priscilla said. "At least for the Gentiles, fathers are like gods to their children. They are absolute rulers."

"For us Jews, too," Aquila added. "Well, not like gods, but the patriarch is the head of the family."

"And Paul is like that to us and to his converts," Timothy concluded. "Therefore, he ought to be respected and honoured as our authority figure."

"But the important part of what I just said," Paul commented, "is not so much my authority as it is that they obey my instructions concerning their behaviour. It is imperative that they have a walk worthy of God because he continuously calls them to live life as it should be lived in his own kingdom and for his glory."

"In other words, they must reflect the character of the one who calls them," Priscilla said.

"Yes," Paul replied, "because God's kingdom is both present and yet to come. It is 'becoming' . . . all things are being renewed, if you will. That is why our Lord taught us to pray, 'Your will be done on earth as it is in heaven.'[19] What Jesus began with his

---

18. See Weima, "Infants," 209–29, https://www.calvin.edu/library/database/crcpi/fulltext/ctj/88086.pdf.

19. Matthew 6:10.

incarnation is something we experience now and, therefore, we ought to live accordingly.[20] And yet, it is something that is still to be completed and, therefore, we ought to live in anticipation of the moment of his unexpected return."[21]

"True," Silas nodded. "God's promise to place all things under Jesus does not appear to have been fulfilled as yet, but we do know that Jesus has been crowned with glory and honour[22] and that he is seated at the right hand of God, reigning as king until all his enemies have been placed under his feet."[23]

"Therefore," Paul began excitedly, "write, Silas! Write this: 'Therefore, we give thanks to God constantly because, having received our message, you welcomed it not as a word of men but, as it is truly, as the word of God which is at work in those of you who are believing. As such, you, brethren, became imitators of the Judean churches of God in Christ Jesus because you suffered the very same things from your fellow countrymen as they did from their countrymen.'"[24]

"Can you pause for just a bit, please?" Silas begged.

"Who are you referring to, Paul?" Aquila asked. "The current purging of the Zealots, or others?"

"Allow me to clarify that. Silas, are you ready?"

Silas nodded as he scribbled the last word.

---

20. Romans 14:17–18; 1 Corinthians 6:9–10; Galatians 5:21; 2 Thessalonians 1:5.

21. 1 Corinthians 15:24, 50.

22. Hebrews 2:9.

23. 1 Corinthians 15:25.

24. As noted before with regard to the possible reason why those who belonged to the party of the Pharisees opposed Paul at the Council of Jerusalem, the reference here to Judean believers suffering at the hands of the Jews may allude to a rising Zealot nationalist movement that took place just prior to the writing of 1 Thessalonians "during the governorship of Tiberius Julius Alexander (AD 46–48) and his successor, Ventidius Cumanus (AD 48–52)." Weima, *1–2 Thessalonians*, 167.

"Those Jews who both killed the Lord Jesus as well as their own prophets and who drove us out, who do not please God and who are hostile towards those they oppose, repeatedly hinder us from speaking to the gentile nations that they may be saved."

"That sounds like something Jesus said just before he foretold the destruction of the temple in Jerusalem," Silas said, looking up suddenly as he recalled the words. "He was addressing the scribes and the Pharisees at the time. He said that they would not escape judgement because they killed and oppressed all the prophets and the wise men God had sent to them, hounding them from town to town . . . in fact, he indicated that they would be held culpable for the cumulative shedding of righteous blood, starting from the killing of Abel to the murder of Zechariah the son of Berekiah, and that judgement for this would be visited upon that very generation."[25]

"That reminds me of what God said to Abraham about the Amorites," Timothy added. "That his descendants would only be freed from bondage once the iniquity of the Amorites was complete."[26]

"Indeed," Paul said soberly, "by their actions, past and present, they are filling up the quota of their sins. And judgement has come on them at last."

"Could we take a quick break, Paul?" Silas asked.

"Yes, I believe our gracious hosts have provided us with some wholesome sustenance."

"Good, because I'm . . ."

"Famished!" Paul and Silas chorused together.

"Leave him be," Priscilla scolded. "He's a growing boy!"

"He will be . . . sideways, if he continues to eat this well!"

---

25. Matthew 23:34–39.
26. Genesis 15:16.

8

Fear versus Faith

Corinth (Acts 18:1–11; 1 Thessalonians 2:17–4:18)

> Paul writes 1 Thessalonians 2:17–4:18. Here he teaches about faith, love, sexual morality, the resurrection of the dead, and the return of Jesus Christ. Paul works closely with his companions in writing his letters to the Thessalonians to offer guidance and encouragement to this early Christian community.

Paul looked out over the city. The flickering of oil lamps and small fires made it look as if thousands of fireflies had converged on the metropolis. The shadows between the various buildings had grown deeper, creating a sharp contrast between light and dark.

"Yes," Paul thought to himself, "an apt image for the spiritual character of the city. Out there, people are seeking the one true God amid deep darkness. It is up to us to introduce him to them."

Because Corinth had two main harbours connected by a four-mile rock-hewn track that enabled cargo and small ships to be hauled across the length of the isthmus, it was an important hub of trade and travel, making the city and many of its inhabitants wealthy. But the city also had a significant proportion of disadvantaged people. Paul had laboured among both segments. Most citizens, whether prosperous or modest, lived side by side, but there was one area that was almost exclusively a neighbourhood for the affluent.[1]

"What a mixed bag of people," Paul thought to himself. He wondered if this financial inequality would later cause problems in the larger community.[2]

The air was alive with chatter and laughter as families and friends enjoyed a bit of downtime together. Footsteps echoed along the narrow streets and alleys as some began to return home, their heads covered to shield them from the bitterly cold winter wind whistling around the corners. Others had gathered at various temples to worship or to beg the gods for intervention. These were not the gods of the Greeks as the inhabitants of the city were mostly Romans. At the centre of the city stood a temple – not for the worship of Aphrodite but Venus.

One temple, intended for the imperial cult, dominated the skyline because its foundations had been built much higher than all the other buildings in the forum area, including the temple of Apollo.[3] Some worshippers carried torches, and the inside light together with the lanterns of the supplicants bathed these Roman podium-style structures in a soft, warm glow, creating an almost mystical ambience against the backdrop of the darkened night sky.

---

1. Keener, *Acts*, 2686–88. See also Garland, *1 Corinthians*, 3–9.
2. 1 Corinthians 11:21–22.
3. Winter, *After Paul Left Corinth*, 9.

"No wonder people are in awe of these false gods," he thought. "The immense temples and shrines, the lifelike statues of heroes, gods, and goddesses, the elaborate rituals, and the mystical priests and priestesses, with their enigmatic omens and dramatic pronouncements . . . all serve to ensnare them and to keep them ensnared."

"I should say something about my hasty departure and my continued absence," commented Paul as he returned from gazing out the window to sit down with the group who were still happily munching on the dried figs and nuts.

"Don't you ever stop eating?" Silas joked, as Timothy shoved one more date in his mouth.

Timothy made a face at Silas as he continued to munch. "I'm a growing boy," he burbled, "ask Priscilla."

"Well, swallow that quickly," Paul said laughing, "we need to get back to that letter if we are going to get any sleep tonight."

"You'll make him choke," Priscilla chided. "Here, Timothy, drink a little wine. It will help you with your digestion."

"Thanks, but no thanks," Timothy answered, swallowing hard. "I only drink water."[4]

"Then drink this barley water. It was boiled, and it won't upset your stomach."

"Come, now," Paul said, sitting down with his back against a warmer inner wall. "Let us continue."

"I'm ready," Silas said, repositioning himself.

"We are starting a new line of thought here, so begin with the word 'but' to signal the change. I also want to structure this section in three units, first addressing my absence, then addressing their current experience of persecution, and then drawing these ideas together with reference to Timothy's report.

---

4. 1 Timothy 5:23.

His going as my representative proves that there is no lack of concern on my part."

"Alright," Silas agreed. "That makes perfect sense."

"So, write this: 'But we, brethren, being orphaned[5] from you briefly . . .'" Paul paused fleetingly and then added, "in person but not in heart, we were very eager to see you, greatly longing for you. Therefore, we wanted to come to you – indeed I, Paul, desired to do so more than once, but Satan made sure our path to you was blocked.'"[6]

"Do you have that, Silas?"

"Yes, yes, you can continue."

"Now, I want to give them the reason why we so longed to see them. Let's see. Hmm . . . write this: 'For who is our hope or joy or crown of boasting before our Lord Jesus Christ at his coming, if not you? For you are at once both our pride and our joy.'"

"I like that," affirmed Timothy. "It assures them that your desire to return was not out of a sense of obligation but because you love them sincerely."

"And it tells them that you are proud of them," Aquila added, "just like a parent would be of their children."

Paul nodded but did not reply. "Let's continue. 'So, when we could no longer endure it, we were pleased to be left alone in Athens and, in our stead, sent Timothy, our brother and fellow worker of God in the gospel of Christ to establish you and to encourage you regarding your faith so that no one should be unsettled by these afflictions.'"

---

5. The Greek word *aporphanizo* should be translated as "orphaned from" as it fits with Paul's previous familial metaphors. See Weima, *1–2 Thessalonians*, 196.

6. This may be a reference to his opponents – viewed here as messengers of Satan – who hounded him, not only out of the city but out of the province.

"Steady on, Paul," Timothy joked. "Those are lofty titles for little me."

"I don't agree," Silas said, pausing for a moment in his writing. "Besides, by assigning such significant status to you, Paul is making it clear that you are no mere messenger but, rather, an extension of himself."

"Precisely." Paul agreed. "But that does not mean I am insincere in what I have said. You are both my representatives when I cannot be present."

"Thank you," Timothy said. "That is very encouraging."

Silas smiled as he continued writing. Ever since Paul had been found wanting in his judgement of John Mark, he had displayed a kinder side, especially when it came to young Timothy.

"Are you ready, Silas?" Paul asked.

Silas nodded, and so Paul continued. "Picking up on the last phrase regarding their afflictions, write this: 'For you yourselves know that to this we are appointed.'"

"True," Priscilla affirmed. "Our faith unavoidably elicits hostility and resistance because it exposes what is false."

"Yes," Paul said, "therefore we need to remind them that even while we were with them, we warned them that we would be afflicted, which is exactly what happened, as they well know. Rewrite that will you please, Silas?"

Silas nodded, and after having reread what he had written, Paul continued. "Therefore, because I was deeply concerned for you, I sent to find out about your faith in case somehow the tempter had led you astray and our labour had thus been in vain."

"Indeed," Timothy agreed solemnly, "if we endure affliction we learn how to persevere.[7] It's like training in the gymnasium.

---

7. See Romans 5:3–4.

It is difficult in the beginning because your muscles ache after every exercise, but as you press on, you develop the strength needed to not back down."

"Exercise has certainly done you no harm, Timothy," Paul acknowledged, "but while physical exercise does have some value, spiritual exercise is much more valuable because it enhances both your present and your future life."[8]

Priscilla laughed. "It's just dawned on me that that's why you're always hungry!"

"It's because of all the exercise, yes," Silas chuckled.

"And so, we press on to the third part of this section of the letter," Paul said, trying to bring them back on track. "But now Timothy has returned to us from you, and he has brought us good news about your faith and your love, assuring us that you remember us fondly too, longing to see us even as we also long to see you. For this reason, we were comforted, brethren, despite our worry and concern over you, to hear about your faith because now we truly live if you continue to stand firm in the Lord. For what thanks are we able to return to God concerning all the joy with which we rejoice because of you before our God? We plead profusely night and day that we might see you all face to face once again to complete the things you still need to learn about your newfound faith."[9]

"Please give me a moment, Paul," Silas said. "That's quite a mouthful."

"Whenever you are ready." Paul closed his eyes and began to pray silently.

---

8. 1 Timothy 4:8.

9. This is my paraphrase of the original, "to complete the things that are lacking in your faith."

After a time of silence, when only the scratching of the nib on parchment could be heard, Paul suddenly stretched out his hands as if to receive an invisible gift and said, "May our God and Father and our Lord Jesus Christ clear the way for us to come to you."

He paused briefly, then added, "And may our Lord cause you to abound and to exceed in love for one another and for everyone else, even as we also grow in our love towards you."

After another pause, Paul continued, "And may he grant you hearts blameless in holiness before our God and Father, in the manifestation of our Lord Jesus Christ, together with all his saints."

"Amen," echoed Aquila, moved deeply by the prayer.

"Amen," they all chorused.

For a few moments, they sat in silence. Then Paul cried, "Amen!" and slapped his hand on his knee. "We must continue while the night is still young."

"Now," said Paul, repositioning himself on a cushion on the floor, "we need to make my final prayer for holiness practical. First, I want to address a problem common to the world they have left behind."

"And what is that?" Silas inquired.

"Sexual immorality."

"That's a common problem to be sure," Priscilla agreed. "In all the Greek and Roman cities, people tend to be very flexible when it comes to sexual activities."

"Indeed," Aquila said gravely, "and some three hundred years ago, one of the Athenian statesmen – apparently considered one of their best orators – once said that men kept mistresses for their enjoyment, concubines for their daily physical needs, and wives to bear legitimate children and serve as reliable caretakers of our households!"[10]

"And attitudes have not changed much," Priscilla added.

"Didn't Cato praise men who had sex with prostitutes rather than with other men's wives?" Silas asked.[11]

"I'm amazed at how familiar you all are with the Greeks," remarked Paul.

"Only a few," Silas admitted."

"And then there's Cicero as well," Aquila added. "He made it clear that men being active with prostitutes was not only legal but consistent with ancient practice!"[12]

"Not to mention the sexual activity connected to the pagan religious rites," Timothy added, blushing ever so slightly. "In fact, the worship of Dionysus is quite popular in Thessalonica."[13]

"And that is why we need to warn our brethren not to fall back into their old pagan ways," Paul said. "Silas, whenever you're ready."

"I'm ready," Silas replied.

---

10. Demosthenes, *Neaer* 59.122, https://www.perseus.tufts.edu/hopper/text?doc=Perseus%3Atext%3A1999.01.0080%3Aspeech%3D59%3Asection%3D122.

11. "Seeing someone he knew exit from one, Cato's noble words were: 'A blessing on all your doings, since it's fine when shameful lust swells youngsters' veins for them to wander down here, and not mess around with other men's wives.'" Horace, *Sat.* 1.2.31–35, https://www.poetryintranslation.com/PITBR/Latin/HoraceSatiresBkISatII.php.

12. "Anyone who thought young men ought to be forbidden to visit prostitutes would certainly be the virtuous of the virtuous, that I cannot deny. But he would be out of step not only with this easy-going age but also our ancestors, who customarily made youth that concession. Was there ever a time when this was not habitual practice, when it was censured and not permitted, in short when what is allowable was not allowed?" Cicero, *Cael.* 48, http://attalus.org/cicero/caelius.html#nr48.

13. See Edson, "Cults of Thessalonica," 153–204.

"Concerning the rest then, brethren," Paul began thoughtfully, "we entreat you and we urge you in the Lord Jesus that even as you heard from us how you should walk and so please God, you strive to do so even more."

He paused for a moment to allow Silas to finish and then added, "For you know what strict instructions[14] we gave you through the Lord Jesus. God wants you to be holy . . ."

"Yes," Timothy interrupted, "holiness is what sets us apart as the people of God."[15]

Paul continued without responding, "God wants you to be holy . . . and that means you must abstain from all forms of promiscuity. That's the first part of my counsel," Paul said, interrupting himself. "Holiness demands abstaining from immoral practices, but it also requires a measure of self-control . . . so, Silas, add this: 'Each one of you must learn how to contain your sexual desires, in purity and honour rather than in self-indulgent licentiousness as is common among the Gentiles who do not know God.'"

"I like that word 'honour,'" Silas said, quill poised over parchment. "It emphasizes respect for the other person."

"Exactly," Paul agreed. "So, add this: 'Make sure that none of you cheats or abuses your brethren in this matter because the Lord will justly punish these things as we explained to you before and solemnly warned you. For God has not called us to uncleanness but to purity. Therefore, whoever despises our counsel does not despise a man but God, who is also the one who gives his Holy Spirit to you.'"

---

14. The Greek word *parangelias* indicates a command given by military or civil authorities.

15. Exodus 19:5-6; Leviticus 11:44-45; 19:2; 20:7, 23-26; 22:32; Deuteronomy 26:18-19.

"Well said!" declared Timothy. "It is important for them to realize that the reason we must desist from depravity is because our bodies are the dwelling place of the Holy Spirit who has taken up residence in us, just as he took up residence in the tabernacle and the temple."[16]

"True," Aquila agreed, "but it is also the Holy Spirit who gives us the ability to overcome temptation and empowers us to live holy lives."[17]

"Yes," said Paul, "so, we have counselled them to live lives that reflect their new faith in a God in whom there is no unrighteousness[18] by abstaining from immoral behaviour, exercising self-control, and respecting the lives of others, but there is an even more important way . . ."

"And that way is?" Priscilla inquired.

"Love. If they love each other, they will not sin against each other."

"But they *do* love one another," Timothy objected. "They demonstrate their love in the way they care for each other – and not only for each other but for everyone in Macedonia."

"Of course," Paul replied, agreed. "So, Silas, write this: 'But concerning your love for each other, there is no need for us to write to you because you yourselves are taught by God to love one another, as indeed you love all the brethren in all of Macedonia.'"

"I like that," Timothy beamed. "However, I must add that there is a minority who makes things difficult for others by meddling in things that don't concern them and by taking advantage of the kindness of others because they don't work themselves."

---

16. Exodus 40:34–38; 2 Chronicles 5:14; 1 Corinthians 6:19.
17. Ezekiel 36:25–27.
18. Psalm 92:15.

"Alright, then let's add this: 'But we exhort you, brethren, to increase in your love more and more and to try earnestly to live quiet lives, to refrain from being busybodies, and to work with your own hands, as we enjoined you, so that you may walk becomingly towards those outside and not be in need of anything.'"

"Brilliant!" Timothy declared. "This way, no one can say you are singling them out."

"And you were an excellent example to them," Silas said, looking up from the parchment for a moment.

"As he is to us all," affirmed Aquila.

"Now," Paul said, closing his eyes once more, "I want to address their question about those who have died. Clearly, we did not give them enough information about the resurrection of the dead and the return of Christ. So, I want to start by ensuring that they know that their beloved departed are safe with Jesus right now. As Jesus told the thief on the cross that he would be with him in paradise at the moment of death,[19] so they need to know that the instant we discard this body – our temporary abode or our tent, if you will – we are present with the Lord.[20] In other words, when Jesus returns, he will bring with him those whom God has already placed with him."[21]

"But what about the discarded body?" Timothy asked. "I think that is more what they are worried about – whether the dead will somehow be at a disadvantage at the return of Jesus. Like souls without bodies."

"So, when I speak about the return of Jesus, I will mention the discarded bodies . . . I will call them the 'dead in Christ' . . .

---

19. Luke 23:42–43.
20. 2 Corinthians 5:8.
21. Ephesians 2:6.

and I will assure them that the souls of those returning with Jesus to the earth will be reunited with their resurrected bodies."

"How will you make this distinction?" Silas questioned.

"I think by using two different words. At first, we will speak about the dead as those who sleep, using this commonly used euphemism for death.[22] And then, when we speak about their dead bodies, we will use the usual word for dead. Does that make sense?"[23]

"And how will you explain the coming of Jesus?" Priscilla asked.

"Like the coming of a conquering emperor," Paul declared. "They all know that the emperor arrives with his entourage and that the folk in the receiving city go out to meet them as he approaches. Then they all enter the city together."[24]

"That's almost exactly like what happened when Jesus entered Jerusalem on the back of that foal!" Silas exclaimed. "His disciples and others who had been with him in Bethany went along with him over the Mount of Olives, and the people in Jerusalem came out of the city to meet him en route, and

---

22. Genesis 47:30; Deuteronomy 31:16; 2 Samuel 7:12; 1 Kings 2:10; 11:43; 22:50; Job 14:12; Psalm 13:3; Isaiah 14:8; 43:17; Jeremiah 51:39; Daniel 12:2. See also Homer, *Il.* 11.241, https://www.perseus.tufts.edu/hopper/text?doc=Perseus%3Atext%3A1999.01.0134%3Abook%3D11%3Acard%3D210; Sophocles, *El.* 509, https://www.perseus.tufts.edu/hopper/text?doc=Perseus%3Atext%3A1999.01.0188%3Acard%3D504; Aelian, *Historical Miscellany*, 2.35, https://www.loebclassics.com/view/LCL486/1997/volume.xml; Cicero, *Sen.* 81, https://www.perseus.tufts.edu/hopper/text?doc=Perseus%3Atext%3A2007.01.0039%3Asection%3D81; Catullus, *Carmina*, 5, https://www.perseus.tufts.edu/hopper/text?doc=Perseus%3Atext%3A1999.02.0006%3Apoem%3D5.

23. This is speculation on my part.

24. Josephus, *Ant.* 2.7.5, 13.4.4, 14.12.2; see also Matthew 25:6, 10 – where the virgins are called to "come out to meet" the bridegroom and then go in with him to the marriage feast – and Acts 28:15.

then they all walked back together . . . the advancing crowd with the returning crowd."

"And so heaven and earth meet again as Jesus returns," Aquila murmured. "Those who were parted from each other will be united once more in a new creation."

There was an awe-filled hush, then the group broke out in spontaneous praises, and it was some time before silence embraced them again.

"So, let us write: 'I do not desire you to be ignorant brethren about those who have fallen asleep[25] in case you grieve as the rest who have no hope.'"[26]

Paul paused, thinking about how best to word his statements. "For if we believe that Jesus died and rose again, so we also believe that God will bring with him those who are asleep in Jesus. Now, this we say to you by a word of the Lord,[27] that those who are still alive at the time of the Lord's return will not take precedence over those who have fallen asleep in Christ."[28]

Paul fell into deep thought again. Then he said, "Because the Lord himself will descend[29] from heaven with a word of

---

25. The Greek verb *koimao* is being used in a figurative sense as a euphemism for death.

26. For an in-depth discussion of life after death in gentile thought, see chapter 2 of Wright, *Resurrection*, 32–84.

27. It is possible that Paul, when writing this part of the letter, had in mind Jesus's words as recorded in Matthew 13:24–30, 37–43, 24:40–41, and 25:1–13.

28. In other words, either both will be transformed at the same time or the dead will be transformed before those who are alive. In 1 Corinthians – a letter written shortly after 2 Thessalonians – Paul states that at the return of Jesus, the dead will be raised incorruptible and we will all – both those who have discarded their bodies and those who are still in their bodies – receive glorified bodies (1 Corinthians 15:51–53).

29. In Greek, *parousia*.

command, by the voice of an archangel and with the trumpet call of God . . ."[30]

"That sounds like when God descended on Mount Sinai," Timothy exclaimed.

"I like that image," Priscilla added.

"Yes," Paul agreed, "I think they will be able to understand the imagery. Now, let's continue . . . with the trumpet call of God, and the dead[31] in Christ . . ."

"So, you want to use the harsh word for death here?" Silas inquired.

"Yes," Paul replied. "The dead in Christ will rise again first,[32] then we who are still living,[33] those who are still on earth, will be caught up[34] together with them in the clouds . . ."

"Yes!" Silas was almost shouting. "Clouds always indicate the coming of God,[35] and that's what the angels told us when Jesus ascended in the clouds – that he would return on the clouds."[36]

---

30. Psalm 47:5; see also Exodus 19:13, 16, 19; 20:18; Isaiah 27:13; Joel 2:1; Zephaniah 1:14–16; Zechariah 9:14; 1 Corinthians 15:51–52.

31. In Greek, *nekroi*, which means "the dead."

32. "Paul believed that the soul lived in heaven till the resurrection of the body and that soul and body would be reunited at the resurrection. See 2 Corinthians 5:1–10." Keener, *IVP Bible Background Commentary*, 589.

33. I do not think that this means that Paul believed in an imminent return. The "we" simply refers to those believers who are alive at the time of Christ's return.

34. The Greek word *arpagesometha* means to be snatched away from danger or removed from one place to another. See Acts 8:39; 2 Corinthians 12:2; Revelation 12:5.

35. Clouds often describe a theophany or the appearance of God. See Daniel 7:13–14 for a description of the ascension – the enthronement and exaltation of the Son of Man – who is shown in Daniel's vision as *coming* to the Ancient of Days, rather than returning from or leaving as at the Parousia. See also Ephesians 1:20–22.

36. Acts 1:9–11.

Paul laughed. "We need to get this letter finished before cockcrow! Let's write now and praise God later. So, continue. 'Caught up together with them in the clouds to a meeting with the Lord in the air,[37] and so we will always be with the Lord. So, then, comfort one another with these words.'"

Aquila yawned. "Paul, this is fascinating and breathtaking, but forgive me, I need to get some sleep tonight."

"Nothing to forgive." Paul stood up immediately. "If Silas and Timothy are agreeable, we can move down to the back of the workshop so that we will not disturb you."

"I will bring down what's left of the refreshments," Priscilla said sleepily, "and then I will join my husband."

"Here, let me help you with those writing materials, Silas," offered Timothy, bundling up some extra quills and sealing the ink pot.

The three men made their way down the stairs into the dark space at the back of the workshop. Paul lit another oil lamp, and soon the room was filled with light. The tang of the tanned leather Paul used to strengthen the corners of his tents hung heavily in the air. The men cleared a space for them to sit as Priscilla handed them each a cup of warm mint-infused barley water. Timothy wrapped a piece of goat-hair cloth around his shoulders as he did not have a cloak.

"It is cold tonight," he complained.

"We need to get you a cloak," said Paul, concerned. "I do not want you to get sick."

---

37. The "air" might be seen as a neutral space between earth and heaven, perhaps used to indicate the lack of advantage one over the other, so that those who have already died are not at a disadvantage.

"I will find some suitable fabric in the morning," said Priscilla, as she began to ascend the stairs, "and make you a cloak that will be the envy of all Corinth."

"That is kind," said Timothy, deeply moved by her gesture. "You are both so kind."

"Hospitality is our gift," Priscilla replied. "And we must use our God-given gifts for the benefit of all, not so? Now, if you will excuse me, I wish you all a pleasant and blessed rest."

"Sleep well," the men replied in unison.

"Now," Paul said, propping himself up against the back wall, "where were we?"

Silas read the last few lines he had written.

"Good. Now let us address their misunderstanding of the timing of our Lord's return, shall we?"

Paul thought for a while and then dictated, "Now, concerning the times and the seasons, brethren, there is no need for us to write to you because you know rightly that the day of the Lord comes as a thief at night."[38]

"I know you taught them well, Paul," Timothy said. "You repeatedly referenced all those passages from the prophets concerning the punishment of the evil and the vindication of the righteous."[39]

"Yes, but from what you told us, it seems their thinking has been muddled by the public indoctrination of the Romans,"[40] put in Silas, looking up briefly from his writing. "Just like the leaders in Jeremiah's day who constantly kept saying, falsely,

---

38. Matthew 24:43; Revelation 16:15.

39. Isaiah 2:1–4:6; Jeremiah 46:10; Ezekiel 30:2–3; Obadiah 15; Joel 1:15; 2:1, 11, 31–32; Amos 5:18–20; Zephaniah 1:14–18; Zechariah 14.

40. "The Romans vigorously promoted themselves as those who secured not only 'peace' but also, though to a lesser degree, 'security.'" Weima, *1–2 Thessalonians*, 349.

'Peace, peace,' as if all was well when it was obvious that there was no peace and all was not well."[41]

"And that has confused them, yes," Paul agreed. "So, write: 'For when they say, "peace and safety," then suddenly destruction will come on them as labour suddenly comes on a pregnant woman[42] and most certainly none will escape.'"

"That is very reassuring for our brethren, to be sure," Timothy mused. "Those who believe in Jesus have everlasting life and will not come into judgement because in him they have already passed from death to life."[43]

"Certainly," Paul concurred, "and they are not in darkness that the day should overtake them as a thief. They are all children of light and children of the day. Write that, Silas, and then add this . . ."

"One moment, please," begged Silas, hastily writing down what Paul had said. "Ready."

"Brethren, we are not of the night nor of the darkness, therefore let us not sleep in spiritual slothfulness[44] like the rest, but let us watch and be vigilant.[45] Because those who sleep, sleep at night, and those who get drunk get drunk at night; but we are of the day. Therefore, let us be serious by putting on a breastplate of faith and love and, as a helmet, the sure certainty of our salvation."[46]

"Is that a quote from Isaiah?" Timothy asked.[47]

---

41. Jeremiah 6:14.
42. Mark 13:8, 33.
43. John 5:24.
44. In Greek, *katheudo*, a word that invokes the idea of apathy.
45. Matthew 24:42–44.
46. Ephesians 6:11–17.
47. Isaiah 59:17.

Paul smiled approvingly. "Yes, your mother and grandmother taught you well.[48] But the reason our Thessalonian brethren can be certain of their salvation is because God has not appointed us to wrath but, rather, for the attainment of salvation through our Lord Jesus Christ, who died on our behalf. So, whether we are alive or dead,[49] we always live together with him. Therefore, they ought to comfort one another and build up one another, as indeed they do."

"Let me rephrase what you said before I write that down." Silas repeated Paul's words and then wrote them down once Paul gave his approval.

"I have a few final words of exhortation for them, and then we can rest," Paul promised. "Are you ready, Silas?"

Silas nodded.

"And we ask you, brethren, to respect those who labour among you, those who lead you in the Lord and who instruct you. Regard them with the utmost esteem in love because of their work. Be at peace among yourselves."

Paul sighed, stifling a yawn, and then added, "And we urge you brethren to reprimand the insubordinate idlers, comfort the faint-hearted, care for those who are weak, and be longsuffering towards all. See that no one returns evil for evil, but always pursue what is best for each other and for everyone else as well. Rejoice always. Pray continually. In everything, give thanks for this is the will of God in Christ Jesus for you. Do not smother the Spirit. Do not despise prophecies but be ready to test all things, accepting only that which is good. Be wary of every form of evil."

---

48. 2 Timothy 1:5.

49. In Greek, the phrase used means whether awake or asleep. I believe that what Paul meant to convey here is that whether we are alive or dead, we are with the Lord.

"I need another quill, please, Timothy."

"I am almost done, Silas," Paul said. "I think we all need to rest now. But allow me to bring this letter to a close."

"Could I perhaps have another light, please?" Silas asked. "I can't see properly any more. I think I'm tired."

"You *think* you are tired?" Paul laughed. "I think you are exhausted. Come, give me the quill and parchment, and I will finish the letter."[50]

Timothy lit another oil lamp and placed it on a stand next to where Paul was squatting.

Paul spoke out loud as he wrote: "And may the God of peace himself purify you fully, and may you be preserved wholly blameless – spirit, soul, and body – at the coming of our Lord Jesus Christ. The one who calls you is faithful, and he will most certainly do this. Brethren, pray for us. Greet all the brethren with a holy kiss.[51] I charge you by the Lord that you read this letter to all believers. The grace of the Lord of us, Jesus Christ, be with you. Amen."

"Amen," Silas and Timothy said solemnly.

"And now," Paul announced, as he carefully returned the parchment to Silas, "it is time for us to rest. Tomorrow is almost today."

---

50. On the practice of an author dictating the letter to a secretary and then writing the closing himself, see Weima, *1–2 Thessalonians*, 429–30.

51. This was a common practice in Middle Eastern and Mediterranean cultures. However, it seems to have become a problem later in the early church. See note 19 in Weima, 426.

9

Resistance and Assistance

Corinth (Acts 18:12–18a)

> Paul plans to send Timothy to deliver a letter to the believers in Thessalonica, and Silas asks to accompany him. Unbelieving Jews continue to oppose Paul's message, but some members of the Corinthian synagogue – including Titius Justus and the synagogue leader, Crispus – choose to follow Christ, leading to the formation of a new faith community. Paul has a profound spiritual encounter, where he sees and hears Jesus, who reassures him and encourages him to continue preaching.

"I thought you would take a break from tentmaking since the gift arrived from Philippi," Priscilla scolded Paul as she came down from the upper room.

Timothy emerged, yawning loudly and scratching his head. "I slept so well, but now I'm . . ."

Before he could finish his sentence, Priscilla thrust a wooden platter filled with bread, cheese, olives, and a few dried figs into his hands.

"Thanks," he said as he took it, surprised. "How did you know?"

"In my defence," said Paul, looking up at Priscilla, "Gaius[1] wanted this tent delivered today."

"Oh, and one cannot refuse Gaius!" Priscilla teased.

"You are joking, I know, but having someone as important as Gaius in our community may prove helpful."

"Well, you have certainly been a consistent witness to him."

"Timothy, are you rested enough to take the letter we wrote to our brethren in Thessalonica?" Paul asked.

"I most certainly am," Timothy mumbled, his mouth full of bread.

"No, he is not," Priscilla objected. "I haven't had time to make that cloak I promised him."

"How long do you need?" Paul asked.

"Two days," Priscilla replied.

"You have one," answered Paul with a grin.

"Cheeky! Besides, he needs a little more mothering. Come, Timothy, I want to buy some fabric. I think wool would be best because it's durable and waterproof. It will be warm and will provide you with good insulation against the cold in Thessalonica."

She put her arm around the young man and dragged him away before there could be any further objections.

"Silas," Paul called.

"I'm awake."

"Get the scroll ready for Timothy to take tomorrow."

---

1. 1 Corinthians 1:14; Romans 16:23.

"Oh, could I go too? I would love to visit our brethren in Philippi, if I may."

"If you like. I have work to do here. I wish to spend more time with our Jewish brethren. Some in the synagogue will poison their minds if I give them half a chance."

"I am discharged of my duty to you!" Paul cried, shaking out his garments in a symbolic gesture.[2] "You have not heeded my warnings. Therefore, your blood be on your own heads. I will no longer be held accountable."[3]

"You are not alone, Paul," said Crispus, pushing his way through the shouting group. "I believe that Jesus is the Messiah!"

"But Crispus," one man shouted, "you are one of the rulers of our synagogue! You cannot leave."

"And I go too," Titius Justus said, going to stand with Paul and some others. "You may bar us from your building, but we will meet in my house."

"That is next door to us," one of the men yelled. "I will not allow it!"

"Try stopping us," challenged Stephanas, also leaving the group, along with his whole family.

"Come, brethren," Paul urged, "if you believe, you must be baptized in the name of the Father, and of the Son, and of the Holy Spirit."

"I know just the place," Stephanas said. "It is a public bath, but quite proper. The water is clean, and the building is often used for lectures."[4]

"May I be baptized too?"

---

2. Nehemiah 5:13.

3. It seems very likely that Paul was alluding to Ezekiel 33:4–9.

4. Keener, *Acts*, 2750.

Paul turned. "Gaius!"

"You are surprised?"

"To see you here, yes! But I am thankful."

"So, what is the answer to my question?"

"Of course, you may, brother! I am surprised it took you this long."

"You have been very patient with me, but I think I knew you were right from the second time we talked together."

"The second time?"

"Yes," Gaius laughed. "But I wanted to know more, so I kept asking you back to my home."

"Then brothers, shall we go to the baths?"

"You will be sorry for this, Paul of Tarsus!" a man shouted as they walked away.

"Then we will meet at my home from now on?" Titius Justus asked.

"You are kind," Paul replied. "May we meet more often than just on the Sabbath?"

"Certainly, I would be honoured."

"Are you alright, Priscilla?" Paul inquired, seeing that she was visibly shaken.

"Yes, I am. It's just that all this unpleasantness reminded me of what happened to us in Rome before Claudius expelled us all."

"I am sorry to have brought up such memories."

"No, no, I realize that if we are to stand for the truth, we ought to expect opposition."

"But this is a happy day, my love," Aquila said, putting his arm around his wife's shoulders. "Look how many the Lord has added to our growing community!"

"Yes," agreed Crispus, "this is a time for rejoicing, not for weeping."

"Here are the baths," Stephanas said. "See, they are fed by an underground spring. It is fresh water."

"I just wish Timothy and Silas were here to witness this." Priscilla suddenly sounded emotional.

"Young Timothy will be home soon enough," Paul reassured her. "In the meantime, why not dote on the children of Crispus and Stephanas?"

"Paul! Paul, are you alright?" Aquila inquired, sounding concerned.

"What?" Paul suddenly became aware of his surroundings once more.

"Are you alright? One moment you were praying, and then you seemed to go into a sort of trance."

After the unpleasant encounter with the unbelieving Jews, Paul had taken a vow not to cut his hair until the church was well established in Corinth,[5] and then he had gathered the brethren together to pray. Their prayer time had been going on for several hours.

"I saw the Lord," Paul said breathlessly.

"The Lord Jesus?" Stephanas was astounded.

"Yes." Paul pointed at the open area opposite him. "He was standing right there."

Crispus gazed at him with his mouth open. "Did he speak to you?" he asked at last.

"Yes. He told me not to be afraid."

"That is surely the most repeated command in the Scriptures," Priscilla added.[6]

---

5. Acts 18:18.

6. The phrase "do not be afraid" is repeated 365 times in the Bible.

"Indeed, but there's more. He said that we should not be afraid to continue speaking . . . that we should not be forced into silence because he is always with us."

"Another oft-repeated phrase," Aquila commented.

"Yes, some of his last words to the disciples just before his return to the Father was to tell us to always remember that he is with us even to the end of the age," Priscilla reminded them. "And that was said in the context of the command to make disciples of all the nations."[7]

"Did he say anything else?" asked Crispus, still dumbfounded by the idea that someone could hear the voice of God.

"Yes, he said that no one will attack us as he has many brethren in this city."

"Many brethren?" Stephanas echoed. "But there is only us . . . a mere handful."[8]

"No, my brother," Paul said, "the Lord knows all who are his own."[9]

"Yes," Priscilla agreed, "Jesus said that his sheep will not listen to the voice of the stranger because they will know the voice of their one, true shepherd."[10]

"That is true," Titius Justus said solemnly, finding his voice at last. "God also told us, through the prophet Isaiah, that we are never to be afraid, since he has redeemed us and called us by name because we are his own."[11]

---

7. Matthew 28:18–20.

8. For a discussion on who these "many people in the city" might have been, see Keener, *Acts*, 2757.

9. 2 Timothy 2:19.

10. John 10:1–18.

11. Isaiah 43:1.

"Does God often speak to you?" Crispus asked. "I know he appeared to you on the road to Damascus and has guided you in dreams, but is it normal for people to hear his voice?"

"I believe Jesus speaks to me when he knows I need more than reassurance. You must remember that I have been stoned and beaten before for preaching the word. I am not made of stone. I am not immune to fear, and the unpleasantness of the other day brought back bad memories."

"We have a prophet among us!" Stephanas cried.

"Not necessarily," Paul responded. "Remember, God has given his Holy Spirit to every one of us, and he gives the Spirit without limitations."[12]

"So, we can all hear his voice?" Crispus asked.

"I believe so," Paul replied. "The sheep hear the voice of their shepherd, as Priscilla correctly reminded us."

"But what does this mean for us, Paul?" Aquila inquired.

"It means we have work to do, brethren. Many more in this city must hear the word!"

---

12. John 3:34; Acts 2:17–18; Ephesians 5:18.

10

Speculation, Signs, and Suffering

Isthmia and Corinth (Acts 18:12–18), Spring AD 51

> In the spring of AD 51, Paul and his companions find themselves caught up in the vibrant atmosphere of the Isthmian Games in Corinth.[1] Timothy shares troubling news from Thessalonica – having returned from there a day earlier – prompting Paul to dictate a letter that would address misunderstandings about the return of Jesus as well the importance of productive employment on the part of believers. The letter emphasizes the importance of remaining steadfast in the face of challenges and holding firm to the teachings they have received.

---

1. The Isthmian Games had recently returned to their original site in AD 50 after having been moved to Sicyon for a century after the destruction of Corinth. See Winter, *After Paul Left Corinth*, 271.

The stadium was alive with the thunder of overexcited crowds of spectators cheering on their favourite athletes from all over the Roman world. The air was filled with the fragrance of olive oil used by the athletes to make their lithe bodies shine in the sunlight and with the sounds of musicians playing to accompany the events. There were so many different events – footraces and chariot races, wrestling and boxing, javelin and discus throwing, and the recitation of poetry and singing. Timothy was surprised to see that women also participated in the games, competing in the footraces and even the chariot races. The champions were celebrated with laurel wreaths and loud praises. It was truly a remarkable experience, a spectacular display of athleticism, culture, and competition, showcasing the spirit and prowess of the contestants.[2]

"So, what did you think of the games?" Paul asked Timothy as the young man returned to the temporary booth Paul had set up with Aquila and Priscilla, with Silas as their helper.

Since there was nowhere to stay at the site, the athletes and participants stayed in tents in the nearby fields. The foursome was so busy fixing and selling tents that they could not attend the games themselves. But Priscilla had insisted that Timothy go. Their presence also afforded them ample opportunities to share the gospel with whoever would stop long enough to listen.

As these games were held in honour of the fearsome god of the sea – called Poseidon by the Greeks and Neptune by the Romans – the message of the crucified Jewish Messiah received mixed responses. It represented a major hurdle for the Jews and seemed like irrational foolishness to the Gentiles.[3] Close by was a temple dedicated to this "divine" patron of the games and, in a smaller building near it, athletes pledged to abide by

---

2. Keener, *Acts*, 2759–60.
3. 1 Corinthians 1:23.

the rules of the games. The punishment for breaking their word was disqualification and disgrace.[4]

"Is there any food to be had?" Timothy asked. "I'm fam . . ."

"Look in the back of the tent," Priscilla interrupted. "Under the netting."

"You didn't answer my question," Paul said, trying to suppress a laugh.

"Oh, it's much more fun participating than watching," said Timothy, breaking open a fresh pomegranate.

"So, why didn't you enter your name for something?" Silas asked jokingly.

"We only just got back a few days ago, and we've been working non-stop to move the workshop from Corinth to here. I didn't have time to adequately prepare myself."

"Excuses, excuses," Silas teased.

"I'll race you back to Corinth," Timothy challenged.

"Carrying all these materials and tents?"

"I think we've made enough money to rent a cart," Priscilla tutted. "Aquila is finding one now. Let him run if he likes. After all, you're only young once."

"You're spoiling him, you know," Paul chided.

"His mother is miles away," Priscilla said defensively.

"You'll make him soft," Silas joking.

"Soft? Me? I'm tougher than you think!"

"Indeed, you are," Paul agreed. "I remember when I was unwilling to let you go off on your own. And now, look at you! Back and forth to Thessalonica on numerous occasions."

"He had company," put in Silas, playfully wrestling a hunk of bread from Timothy's grasp.

---

4. Gordon Franz, "Going for the Gold: The Apostle Paul and the Isthmian Games," *Shiloh Excavations*, 16 July 2012, https://biblearchaeology.org/research/contemporary-issues/3009-going-for-the-gold-the-apostle-paul-and-the-isthmian-games.

"Only until we parted company," Timothy replied, tearing off the larger share of the bread.

"Boys, boys," Priscilla fussed, "there is enough for everyone. You shouldn't be fighting over food."

"He started it," Timothy responded.

"And you're always stuffing your face," Silas teased.

"But he's a . . ." Priscilla began.

"A growing boy! Yes, so you keep reminding us," said Paul, packing some tools in a bag. "But at this rate, he will soon begin to grow sideways."

"Now you are repeating yourself, Paul," Priscilla teased.

"Only because you don't hear and obey," he joked.

"Women always only hear what they want to hear," she shot back.

"I have procured an ox-drawn cart," Aquila said, poking his head around the tent flap. "The driver will be here any moment now, so let's get cracking, shall we?"

"Are you sure they think that this false claim comes from me?" Paul asked exasperated.

As they walked back from Isthmia to Corinth, Timothy had given Paul a full report of what he had seen and heard while in Thessalonica.

"Yes, I'm sure," Timothy replied.

"But how? Through a prophetic utterance? Is someone twisting my words? Or was it a letter purporting to be from me?"

"They wouldn't say."

"Well, we will certainly need to address this in another letter. We cannot have them upset by thinking Jesus has already returned!"

"I agree," Silas said. "As soon as we are settled, I will gather the necessary writing materials."

"But how will you help them understand?" Timothy asked. "There are no signs or indicators as to when the end will be, so how will they know for certain that Jesus has not returned? Jesus clearly taught that no one would know when that day and that hour would be . . . not even the angels know.[5] He said it wasn't for us to know times and seasons.[6] He taught that the wheat and the weeds would grow together until the end when the weeds would be plucked up and cast into the fire.[7] That the wicked would go on being wicked but the righteous would become more holy."[8]

"We will see how the Spirit leads us," Paul reassured him. "He will make it clear."

"Is this going to be another long night?" Priscilla sounded concerned. "Because Aquila is exhausted."

"We do not need to disturb you," Paul assured her. "We can stay down in the workshop."

"Don't you ever get tired?"

"Me? Often. But if I don't write this letter now, I won't sleep tonight!"[9]

Once more the three men prayed for wisdom and guidance in the writing of the letter. They sang praises to the God they adored and confessed their dependence on him. They thanked him for what he had done in Thessalonica and acknowledged that he alone knew what would be best for them. They brought before him all their concerns about the welfare of their brethren

---

5. Mark 13:32–37.
6. Acts 1:7.
7. Matthew 13:30.
8. Daniel 12:10; Revelation 22:11.
9. 2 Corinthians 11:27.

everywhere but asked especially for his intervention in the lives of their persecuted and frightened brethren. After they had sung a hymn of praise, they stood silent for a while, hands outstretched expectantly.

"I would like for us to follow a similar structure to that of our first letter," Paul said as the three men made themselves comfortable.

Once again, Priscilla had ensured that they had enough to sustain them through the writing of the letter.

"Shall I be the scribe this time?" Timothy asked.

"I don't see why not," Silas replied. "I will be the keeper of the quills and scrolls then."

"I want to include your names," Paul said, "because I want to show that we are united in thought and that I am well-informed concerning what has and is happening in Thessalonica."

"I am ready, Paul," Timothy spoke with a quill poised in mid-air.

"So, write: 'Paul, Silvanus, and Timothy, to the church . . .'"

Paul paused. "That word 'church' is important. It's the same word used in the Greek translation for the people of God.[10] I want them to know that there is continuity between them and what has gone before . . ."

"I have it."

"To the church of the Thessalonians, in God our Father and the Lord Jesus Christ."

"That's important too," Silas interjected, "because they need to realize that their origin is in God. That will be comforting to them as they weather this ongoing persecution."

"Correct," agreed Paul. "So, we add, for the same reason, 'Grace to you and peace from God our Father and the Lord

---

10. Greek *ekklesia*, meaning "church."

Jesus Christ.' To show that God is still involved in their everyday lives as his people."

"God is in their past, their present, and their future," Silas mused.

"Now, let's begin by encouraging them. We do not wish to add to their burdens by addressing the complications first. Positive first, problems later. So, we will begin by commending them and then we will comfort them, and only later will we confront them and correct them."

"That's kind," Timothy said. "They really are quite remarkable, you know, given that they are so young in the Lord."

Paul continued. "We ought always to give thanks to God for you, brethren, as is right, because your faith is growing abundantly and the love of every one of you for one another is increasing." He paused to ask, "Do you have that?"

". . . one another is increasing. Yes, I can write just as fast as Silas can, you know!"

"Don't encourage him," Silas warned, laughing. "He will string together those long sentences that will make your hand cramp!"

"I haven't finished my sentence yet!"[11]

"You see?"

"I'm ready."

"Therefore, we ourselves boast about you in the churches of God for your steadfastness and faith in all your persecutions and in the afflictions that you are enduring."

"That is most encouraging, Paul," Silas said. "There is nothing like a parent praising a child to boost confidence. It will also help them, later in the letter, to remember that you are not disappointed in them."

". . . afflictions that you are enduring. Yes?"

---

11. In Greek, the thanksgiving section is two lengthy sentences.

"This is a clear token of the righteous judgement of God, that you may be considered worthy of the kingdom of God, for which you are also suffering."

Paul paused.

"Now, how shall I put this? I want to remind them that God is not indifferent to their suffering and that he will vindicate them in the end."

"You mean what is the evidence of his righteous judgement?"

"Yes."

"Well, how about this: 'Since God indeed deems it just to repay with affliction those who afflict you . . .'"

"That's good," Paul encouraged.

"And to grant respite to you who are suffering . . ."

"as well as to us . . ." Paul added.

"At the unveiling[12] of our Lord Jesus from heaven, together with his powerful angels, who will, then, as in purifying[13] flames of fire,[14] exact retribution on those who do not know God and on those who do not obey the gospel of our Lord Jesus."

"Very good, very good, Silas. Did you get that Timothy?"

"Just a minute . . . yes, I have it." Timothy read back what he had written.

"Excellent." Paul nodded, then continued, "Now write: 'They will pay the penalty of eternal destruction, forever removed from the presence of the Lord as well as from the glory of his power when he comes to be glorified in his saints and to be venerated by all who have believed on that day because you believed our testimony to you.'"

---

12. In Greek, *apokalypseis*, meaning "revelation."

13. The word "purifying" is not in the Greek text, but it helps to explain the imagery.

14. 2 Peter 3:7, 10, 12.

"That is a choice they have made themselves," Silas said gravely. "If they did not choose him in this life, they will not choose to spend eternity with him either."

Paul nodded. He paused for a moment, eyes closed, then added, "For which indeed we always pray concerning you, that our God may consider you worthy of the calling and that he may fulfil every determination for integrity and every work of faith by his power so that the name of our Lord Jesus may be glorified in you, and you in him, according to the grace of our God and the Lord Jesus Christ."

"Amen," Silas said softly.

Again, Paul paused for a while before continuing to dictate, his eyes closed in prayerful concentration, his hand moving in the air as if writing. "Now, brethren, concerning the return[15] of our Lord Jesus Christ and our gathering together to him,[16] we ask you not to be quickly shaken in mind or panicked, either by a prophetic utterance,[17] or a teaching, or even a letter claiming to be from us saying that the day of the Lord has come."

Paul paused again. "I want to tell them that just as our ancestors had to linger long in Egypt until the sins of the Amorites warranted their destruction,[18] so we, too, live in a period of waiting for the sinfulness of humanity to reach a point of no return."

"Or like the time between God's command for Noah to build the ark and the actual flood?" Silas suggested.

---

15. In Greek, *parousia*.
16. 1 Thessalonians 4:17.
17. Literally "through a spirit."
18. Genesis 15:16.

"Yes," Timothy said excitedly. "We are living in a time that mirrors the time of Noah! Just as everyday life went on as usual, people will be taken unawares by the return of Jesus!"[19]

"We live in faith that he will do as he promised," Silas added enthusiastically. "We don't need signs, not when we have his sure word that he knows the time and that he knows what is best. We know he always works all things together for our good!"[20]

"We live in hope," Timothy inserted, "a hope that is certain even though it is not seen!"[21]

"Or *especially* because it is not seen!" Silas said. "Wanting to know all things is what tripped up our first parents![22] It smacks of a lack of trust."

"Silas!" Paul exclaimed. "That's brilliant! Timothy, write, 'Do not allow anyone to deceive you in any way, because[23] this

---

19. Matthew 24:37–39.
20. Romans 8:28.
21. Romans 8:24–25.
22. Genesis 3:6.

23. I have struggled with the translation of this text since, in 1 Thessalonians 5:1–3, Paul seems to indicate that there will be no sign of the end – which is in keeping with Jesus's own statements regarding that day and that hour (Matthew 24:36; Acts 1:7). For this reason, I believe Paul is alluding to the Old Testament understanding of withholding judgement until something is complete or fulfilled. Abraham was told that his descendants would be enslaved until the sins of the Amorites had become so great that they had reached a point of no return (Genesis 15:16). The wicked people during the time of Noah had a period of "grace" up to the point when the ark was shut (Matthew 24:37–39). The false and impotent gods of Pharaoh were eventually exposed after ten plagues and the parting of the Red Sea. The unbelieving generation had forty years of wandering in the wilderness. The exiles had to wait seventy years in Babylon. These are not signs per se but, rather, periods of grace. The context of both 1 and 2 Thessalonians does not present the end in terms of signs like wars, tumult, pestilence, plagues, and famine (which were signs of the destruction of Jerusalem in AD 70) but, rather, as a period of "peace and safety" (1 Thessalonians 5:3).

day will not come before the rebellion[24] and the lawlessness of mankind[25] are exposed[26] – those destined for destruction,[27] who oppose and exalt themselves against every form of godliness,[28] taking for themselves the place that is rightfully God's.'"[29]

"The original sin of Adam and Eve," Silas murmured. "They wanted to be like God, to take his place. But this is a flaw that has been passed on down through the ages to all humanity. I'm thinking particularly about Isaiah's statement concerning the king of Babylon who wanted to exalt himself

---

24. Or apostasy.

25. In Greek, *ho Anthropos tes hamartias*, meaning "the man of sin." Grammatically, the genitive could just be a descriptive genitive – that is, an adjective – and *anthropos* can certainly mean humankind. Hence my translation "the lawlessness of mankind." I believe that this is not an individual but a generic use of the word to include all humanity – in other words, "man" ought to be capitalized. See Louw and Nida, *Greek-English Lexicon*, 9.1, 104. Another view is that "Paul may be speaking of the attitude of people in general (1 John 2:18, 22; 4:3; 2 John 7)." Koudougueret, "2 Thessalonians," in *The Africa Bible Commentary*, 1492. However, I do not agree with the rest of what the author of this commentary says regarding the so-called rapture. For a further explanation of my position, see the appendix.

26. Exposed, uncovered, or revealed. I believe this is a reversal of God covering Adam's sin. Like the sins of the Amorites had to reach a point that warranted destruction, so lawless humanity is finally exposed. The wicked and the righteous continue to live together until the end (see Matthew 13:24–30; Revelation 22:11).

27. In Greek, *ho uios tes apoleias*, meaning "the son of perdition," a term only used here and in John 17:12, where it is used in reference to Judas. I think that Paul is referring to the time when God's patience with the vessels of wrath prepared for destruction (Romans 9:22) runs out.

28. In Greek, *ho antikeimenos kai huperairomenos epi pan to legomenon theon e sebasma*, meaning "he who opposes and exalts himself against every so-called god and form of worship." This sounds very much like a modern secular humanist.

29. Literally "sitting in the temple of God, proclaiming himself to be God."

above God.[30] Throughout history, there have been people who thought themselves above God, like Pharaoh, the Babylonian kings, Antiochus Epiphanes, Herod, the Caesars and especially Caligula, to mention only a few."

"Well done, Silas!" Paul smiled as he opened his eyes. "Yes, I strung together thoughts from several passages in my statement – from Genesis, Exodus, Isaiah, and Daniel, as well as our Lord's own teaching about the end. I did so because that's what I taught them when we were with them, remember? I took them through the Torah and the Prophets."

"I remember, but I wonder if they do," Silas said.

"So, let's ask them! Timothy, are you keeping up with me?"

"Yes, I'm ready."

"So, write, 'Do you not remember that when I was still with you, I told you these things? And you know what is delaying[31] this now so that the uncovering might take place at the right time. For the mystery of lawlessness is already at work.'"

"Is this the work of the Archangel Michael?" Silas was intrigued. "You taught us that he is the protector of God's people, did you not?"[32]

"Yes, that is true, but whoever the agent may be, Silas, the truth remains that it is God's grace that keeps the final judgement at bay. Only now, he holds back[33] judgement and

---

30. Isaiah 14:12–15.

31. In Greek, *antikeimenos*, meaning, "restraining," "resisting," or "opposing." Louw and Nida, *Greek-English Lexicon*, 39.18, 495.

32. Daniel 10:13, 21; 12:1.

33. Or "restrains." The identity of the one who is restraining is hotly debated among New Testament scholars. If Paul had Daniel 10–12 in mind, the restraining thing or person may be the Archangel Michael. See Weima, *1–2 Thessalonians*, 532. Nevertheless, it is still the patient grace of God that keeps judgement at bay, regardless of the agent of such judgement. See 1 Peter 3:20.

will do so until the moment when[34] the lawless are exposed, whom the Lord Jesus will consume with the breath of his mouth[35] and bring to nothing by the appearance of his coming."

"It is our adversary who blinds them," Silas commented. "Jesus said he was a murderer and a liar even from the beginning."[36]

"The action of Satan has always been to deceive those who are perishing," Paul replied, "with all power and false signs and wonders because they do not accept and love the truth so that they might be saved. For this reason, God sends them a strong delusion[37] so that they may embrace what is false . . . so that all who do not believe the truth but, rather, delight in unrighteousness may be judged."

A sombre stillness descended on the group as they pondered this awful reality.

"That is so tragic," Timothy remarked, breaking the silence.

"True," Silas agreed, "but it is also a cause for humble gratitude on our part."

"Indeed," Paul said, suddenly animated. "So, Timothy, write once more: 'But we ought to thank God always for you, you who are our brethren beloved by the Lord, because God chose you from the start for salvation, in sanctification by the Spirit and belief in the truth, having called you through our gospel to acquire the glory of our Lord Jesus Christ. So then, brethren,

---

34. Literally, "it comes out of the midst."

35. Perhaps a reference to the flaming fire in 1 Thessalonians 1:7b.

36. John 8:44.

37. Note the striking resemblance to Romans 1:24 25: "Therefore God gave them over in the sinful desires of their hearts to sexual impurity for the degrading of their bodies with one another. They exchanged the truth about God for a lie, and worshipped and served created things rather than the Creator – who is for ever praised" (NIV).

stand firm and hold to the traditions which you were taught by our spoken word and by our letter.'"

Paul waited for Timothy to catch up. "And may our Lord Jesus Christ himself, and our God and Father, he who loves us and gives us everlasting reassurance and good hope through grace, may he reassure your hearts and may he establish you in every good word and work."

After another pause, Paul added, "Finally, brethren, pray for us, that the word of the Lord may be well received[38] here as it was with you, and pray that we may be delivered from perverse and evil people. For not all believe.[39] But the Lord is faithful, and he will establish you and will protect you against the evil one. And we are persuaded that, with the Lord's aid, you are doing and will do whatever we instruct you. May the Lord guide your hearts to the love of God and the patience of Christ."

For a while all that was heard was the scratching of the quill on the parchment.

They were all tired by this time and in need of a good night's rest. But Timothy spoke up. "We still need to address the idlers among them, Paul. They are wearing out even the most gracious by their opportunistic scrounging."

"So we must!" Paul declared. "Let's say this: 'And we command you, brethren, in the name of our Lord Jesus Christ, that you draw back from anyone who is insubordinate and who does not follow the tradition that you received from us.'"

"I say, Paul, isn't that a bit harsh?" Silas said, taken aback. "Must they shun fellow believers?"

"Well, think about it, Silas," Paul replied patiently. "These people are taking advantage of the kindness of others while they ought to be imitating us . . . we were not indolent among them,

---

38. Literally "run and be glorified."
39. Or "not all have faith."

nor did we take advantage of anyone,[40] but we worked hard by night and by day so as not to burden any of them."[41]

"It is not that they are unable to work, Silas," Timothy interjected. "They don't *want* to work, and they expect other hard-working people to provide for them. They are bored and lazy, and so they cause trouble by meddling in the affairs of others and spreading idle gossip. They think themselves self-important . . . that because of their position in society they have authority to make demands and that they are deserving of such self-indulgence."

Paul nodded approvingly, "Write this, Timothy: 'We are not saying that *we* lack authority . . .'"[42]

"Ha!" Timothy snorted. "That ought to get their attention."

"We are not saying that we lack authority, but we set you an example to imitate by the way we conducted ourselves. Even while we were with you, we told you that if anyone is not willing to work, let him not eat. For we hear that some among you are freeloaders, not keeping busy – providing for yourselves or for others[43] – but being meddlesome. We instruct and exhort such people in the Lord Jesus Christ to earn what they eat themselves and to mind their own business."

"But what if everyone now refrains from helping others?" Silas asked.

---

40. Or "nor did we eat anyone's bread as a gift."

41. However, see 1 Corinthians 9:3–7. He chose not to accept financial aid from the Thessalonians but he did defend his right to be supported as an apostle.

42. It is possibly the idle rich who refused to work. See 1 Thessalonians 4:10b–12; 5:14; 2 Thessalonians 3:6, 10.

43. See 2 Corinthians 9:8–15.

"Good point. So, let's add this: 'As for you, brethren, do not be discouraged from doing good.'[44] And now add, 'If anyone does not obey our counsel in this letter, mark that person and do not associate with them that they may be humbled. However, do not regard them as enemies but warn them as brethren.'"

"In other words, we want to change behaviour or at least encourage good behaviour," Silas stated.

"And with that, let me encourage us to behave well towards our own bodies!" Paul groaned. "My body is aching and cries out for a soft place to rest."

"Would you like to end the letter, Paul?" Timothy asked, holding out the quill and parchment.

"Yes. Thank you, my son. You have done well."

He carefully took the parchment from Timothy's hands, speaking aloud as he wrote, "Now may the Lord of peace himself continuously grant you peace in every way. The Lord be with all of you. Now, as a sign of authenticity in all my letters, I, Paul, write this farewell with my own hand. This is the way I write. The grace of our Lord Jesus Christ be with you all."

"Amen," Silas and Timothy said.

"Amen, and goodnight," said Paul as he handed the parchment back to Timothy.

---

44. Professional freeloaders can discourage people from being kind to those who are truly in need.

11

Time to Travel

Return to Antioch (Acts 18:18b–22)

> Gaius introduces Paul to Phoebe, a new disciple of Jesus. A group of unbelieving Jews arrive and drag Paul before the tribunal, accusing him of misleading people and teaching things contrary to the law. However, the proconsul dismisses the accusations, refusing to intervene in what he sees as a religious matter. After several days, Paul decides to depart from Corinth, entrusting the leadership of the local believers to Gaius, Crispus, and Sosthenes. He plans to return to Antioch, after first stopping over in Jerusalem to report to the church there. Before leaving, Paul had his head shaved at Cenchreae in fulfilment of a vow he had taken earlier.

"Good morning," Gaius called out to Paul. A well dressed woman walked silently by his side.

"Not so loud, Gaius," Paul replied laughing. "Remember Proverbs? A loud greeting in the early morning will be thought of as a curse!"[1]

Gaius roared with laughter. "What, young Timothy still asleep, and you stitching tents all on your own?"

"I'm awake," called Timothy, emerging from the darkness in the back of the workshop.

"Hush, my brother," Paul chided. "Our hosts are still sleeping. They are still exhausted from the trip."

"Too late," a gruff voice said from above. "I will be down shortly. Timothy, please offer our guests some refreshments."

"Will do!"

"So, aren't you going to introduce us?" Paul asked mid-stitch.

"Oh! Yes, I'm so sorry. This is Phoebe from Cenchreae. She is a good friend of the family and now a fellow believer."

Paul stood to greet the newcomer. She was a younger woman with fashionably curly hair tied back with a long piece of cloth. "A believer you say?"

"Yes," Phoebe replied. "Gaius never missed an opportunity to speak to me about Jesus."

"We've known each other for years," Gaius continued, "initially as business associates, but then later we became good friends."[2]

"I have also not been idle since I first believed," Phoebe added. "A number of my friends in Cenchreae now believe, and we meet regularly at my home to study the Scriptures."

"You have scrolls at home?"

---

1. Proverbs 27:14.

2. Some scholars believe that Phoebe was a wealthy business woman, perhaps even managing or owning a fleet of ships, which would explain why she was able to carry Paul's letter to the Roman church.

"A few. My late husband collected several copies on his travels."

"I would love to see them, if I may."

"You are more than welcome."

"May I come too?" Silas said, stepping out into the sunlight.

"Silas!" Gaius stepped forward to embrace and kiss him on both cheeks.

"Here, I've poured enough for all."

"What is it?" Phoebe asked, eyeing the brew suspiciously.

"It is barley water with mint," Timothy explained, smiling. "Priscilla always keeps some on hand. It is very refreshing, either warm or cold."

"Forgive me for not being here to greet you," called out Priscilla, coming down the steps. "We had quite a journey yesterday."

"The games?" Gaius asked.

"Yes, we sold and repaired tents there."

"So, it was a productive journey?" Phoebe asked, ever the businesswoman.

"Oh very," Priscilla enthused.

"I do apologize for waking you up," said Gaius, stepping forward to greet Priscilla properly. They suddenly became aware of the sound of an approaching, raucous crowd.

"Well, if you didn't wake us, that noisy rabble would have!"

"They do sound angry, don't they," Gaius agreed.

"Uhm, Paul," Timothy sounded worried. "I think they are headed this way."

Before any of the friends knew what was happening, Paul was wrenched up and dragged off by a group of unbelieving Jews. Paul's ongoing ministry in Corinth for more than a year and six months had divided the community, and they were afraid that things would only get worse. Even though the bema[3] was not far – being located on the southern edge of the forum at the end of their row of shops – Paul was cut and bleeding by the time they stood before the tribunal.[4]

Gallio,[5] the consumptive older brother of Seneca the younger, had just become proconsul of Achaia, and this delegation of Jews took full advantage of his recent arrival. But they had not reckoned with the fact that the proconsul would be ill-tempered due to his malady. Like Priscilla and Aquila, a loud voice was the last thing he wished to hear that morning.

"This man," they shouted, shoving Paul forward roughly, conveniently neglecting to say anything about Paul's Roman citizenship, "is misleading people, teaching them to worship God in a manner that conflicts with the law."[6]

Paul was not about to submit to another illegal beating, but before he could say anything in his defence, Gallio shot up a hand, angrily demanding silence.

"Stop!" he roared, grimacing at the loudness of his own voice. "If it were a felony or even a political crime, O Jews, then I would have reason to tolerate your protest. But this is yet another one of your endless wranglings about words and names and your own law, and so it is a matter for you yourselves to deliberate. I simply refuse to listen to your whining!"

---

3. As there was a beating at the end of this failed attack, it is probable that this bema was outdoors rather than indoors. Therefore, the likely location was probably the bema – discovered by archaeologists in 1935 – on the southern edge of the forum.

4. Keener, *Acts*, 2764.

5. Bruce Winter, "Rehabilitating Gallio and his Judgement in Acts 18:14–15." *Tyndale Bulletin* 57, no. 2 (2006): 291–308.

6. It may be that the accusers left it unclear which law they meant – Jewish law or Roman law. But it is more likely that they wished to deprive Paul of the privileged status enjoyed by the Jews at that time.

At a motion of his hands, his lictors[7] descended from the elevated platform and forcibly drove the accusers back, allowing Paul to slip away unnoticed.

But the gentile crowd then began to vent their anti-Jewish feelings on Sosthenes, the ruler of the Jews, beating him openly before the tribunal.

"Gallio is doing nothing to stop them," protested Paul, as Priscilla hastily wiped some blood off his forehead.

"We must do something," Gaius said. "Sosthenes is a good man and is close to becoming one of us."[8]

"Then why was he with this angry delegation?" Silas asked.

"I don't know, perhaps to make sure they did not go too far. But now we must stop this injustice."

Without another word, Gaius walked forward boldly to where Sosthenes was lying, arms in the air in a vain attempt to prevent the blows from hitting his head. The mob recognized Gaius as a high-ranking official and backed off.

Gallio had retreated after suffering another of his coughing spells, and so the patrons and clients in the forum had also dispersed.

"Come, brother," Gaius said, gently helping Sosthenes up from the ground.

"Bring him to the shop," Priscilla said.

"Paul," Sosthenes called out feebly, "forgive me. I did try to stop them, but they would not listen."

---

7. Lictors were attendants or guards who accompanied magistrates and did their bidding. They were usually "armed" with an axe protruding from a bundle of birch or elm rods about 1.5 metres long, tied together with a red strap.

8. It is possible that the Sosthenes mentioned in 1 Corinthians 1:1 is the same person.

"No matter, brother," Paul said, still quite shaken by the whole ordeal. "We must get you cleaned up. That was quite a beating they gave you."

"I do believe Jesus is the Messiah, the Son of God," Sosthenes said, spitting blood.

"I know, Gaius told me. Why did you not come to us earlier?"

"I was hoping to persuade the others, but this has destroyed any hopes I had about them."

"God is gracious, brother. Do not give up on them. God may yet turn their hearts."

"Here," Priscilla took Sosthenes by the arm and led him to a place in the shade. "Drink this."

"Are you alright, Phoebe?" Timothy asked. "You are quite pale."

"I am fine, but I could do with a drink of that refreshing barley water," she said with a smile.

"It is time for me to leave," Paul told the brethren after several days had passed. He had wanted to stay long enough to see that the unbelieving Jews did not present any further threat to the fledgling church in Corinth.

Silas and Timothy had left for Thessalonica the day before, planning to retrace their steps through Thessalonica, Philippi, Troas, and on to Lystra, where Timothy would be reunited with his grandmother and his mother. Silas then planned to return to Jerusalem.

"There are now enough of you who can lead the flock. Phoebe, I place you in charge of our community in Cenchreae. Gaius, Crispus, and Sosthenes, you will continue to lead here. Priscilla and Aquila have expressed a desire to accompany me as far as Ephesus, but my aim is to return to Antioch. I plan to report to the church in Jerusalem first. These are two communities that have your best interests at heart."

"You remain in our hearts, Paul," Gaius said, stepping forward and embracing his friend.

"You have brought us life," Sosthenes said, wiping away a tear. "How can we ever repay you?"

"Repay me by remaining faithful to our Lord," Paul replied. "Never stop preaching the word, whether it is accepted or rejected. Teach the flock, especially the new believers. Exhort them, admonish them, and encourage them gently, lovingly, patiently, and carefully."

Aquila had hired a cart to take them to the harbour in Cenchreae, and as they followed it out of the city, Paul turned to Phoebe, "Is there a good barber in Cenchreae?

"I've never used one, but I'm sure there must be. Why?"

"I need to shave my head. My vow has ended."

Short Biographies

Paul – Also known by his Hebrew name Saul (Acts 13:9), Paul was born (around AD 5) a Roman citizen in Tarsus[1] to a family of tentmaking (Acts 18:3) Pharisees (Acts 23:6) of the tribe of Benjamin (Philippians 3:5). We know nothing more about his family other than that he had a married sister and a nephew in Jerusalem at the time of his arrest in that city (Acts 23:16). Paul was educated "according to the strict manner of the law" in Jerusalem under Gamaliel (Acts 22:3 ESV) – grandson of the great Hillel – and, following the martyrdom of Stephen, became the leading persecutor of the early church. On his way to Damascus to arrest believers in that city, Paul met the risen Jesus (around AD 35). Subsequently, the Lord commissioned him to be a witness for the gospel. Paul spent about three years in Arabia, after which he returned to Damascus – but he was forced to leave under cover of darkness due to the negative response to his preaching to the unbelievers in the city (2 Corinthians 11:32–33; Acts 9:22–25). At first, Paul was not well received in Jerusalem because, as a former persecutor, people did not trust him. After Barnabas vouched for him, Paul met with Peter and Jesus's brother James (Galatians 1:18–19). Because of further violent threats, the church in Jerusalem thought it best that Paul return to Tarsus, where he apparently spent several years witnessing in Cilicia and Syria (Acts 9:30; 15:41; Galatians 1:21). As the church in Antioch was fast becoming an ethnically mixed community of believing Jews and Gentiles, Barnabas brought Paul to serve in Antioch. It was in Antioch that the Holy Spirit

---

1. Tarsus was well known for raising goats that produced a high-quality goat-hair cloth that was used for tentmaking.

spoke clearly to the leadership of the church, setting Barnabas and Paul aside for missionary work elsewhere. Three major mission trips are documented in Scripture, but it is possible that after his release from the imprisonment (about AD 60–62) recorded in the closing chapter of the book of Acts, Paul went to Spain as he had planned (Romans 15:23–28).[2] According to Tertullian, Paul was beheaded under Nero's persecution that took place after the great fire of Rome in AD 64.[3]

Aquila and Priscilla – The couple were early Christian converts presently from Rome. It is possible that they may have been converted on the day of Pentecost (Acts 2:5–11). Due to an edict of Emperor Claudius, all Jews, including Jewish believers in Jesus, were expelled from Rome around AD 49, as a result of which this couple moved to Corinth, where they later met Paul. As Aquila and Priscilla were also in the tentmaking trade, Paul lodged with them for about eighteen months before they all moved to Ephesus. There, this couple is said to have corrected inadequate teaching by Apollos (Acts 18:24–26), a well-educated and eloquent Jewish Christian from Alexandria. The couple are mentioned together six times in Scripture (Acts 18:2–3, 18, 26; Romans 16:3–5; 1 Corinthians 16:19; 2 Timothy 4:19) and, significantly, in four of those places, Priscilla's name is mentioned first. This unconventional order of giving the wife's name before her husband's may indicate that Priscilla's ministry was more prominent or active than Aquila's or that she was from a higher-ranking social position. After the death of Claudius

---

2. 1 Clem. 5:5–7; The Muratorian Canon 34–39; Cyril of Jerusalem, *Catechesis*, Lecture 17.26; Chrysostom, *Second Timothy*, Homily 10; Jerome, *Amos*, cap.5;

3. Tertullian, *Scorp.* 15:4; Tertullian, *Praescr.* 36; see also 1 Clem. 5:5–7; Ign. *Eph.* 12:2; Pol. *Phil.* 9:1–2; Dionysius of Corinth (Eusebius, *Hist. eccl.* 2.25.4); Irenaeus, *Haer.* 3.1.1; *Acts Paul*.

in AD 54, it is possible that Priscilla and Aquila were able to return to Rome (Romans 16:3-5). Various traditions state that Paul made Aquila a bishop[4] and that the couple were martyred in Rome under Nero.

Silas – Silas, also called Silvanus (2 Corinthians 1:19; 1 Thessalonians 1:1; 2 Thessalonians 1:1; 1 Peter 5:12) – was a Jewish believer who appears to have been a leader in the Jerusalem church (Acts 15:22, 32). He was also a Roman citizen (Acts 16:37). After the conclusion of the Jerusalem Council, Silas was sent to Antioch, along with Judas Barsabbas, Barnabas, and Paul, to confirm the Council's favourable decision. When Paul and Barnabas decided to go their separate ways – because of an argument concerning John Mark – Paul chose Silas to accompany him on a missionary trip through Syria and Cilicia (Acts 15:40-41), then on to Asia Minor, Macedonia and Greece. Timothy joined the group in Lystra, as did Luke in Troas (Acts 16:1-10). In Philippi, following an exorcism, Paul and Silas were arrested, beaten, and imprisoned. In jail, they were praying and singing hymns to God when an earthquake caused at least a partial collapse of the jail. The unnamed jailer – though initially fearful for his life – was converted, together with his family. When the city officials learned that Paul and Silas were Roman citizens, they were afraid because they realized that they had violated Roman law (Acts 16:19-26).[5] They apologized and immediately released Paul and Silas. Silas and Timothy travelled with Paul from Philippi to Thessalonica, where they were met with resistance in the synagogues by some traditional Jews, who even followed them to Berea, where many Jews and

---

4. *Apos. Con.* 7.46.

5. The *Lex Porcia* exempted Roman citizens from degrading forms of punishment such as whipping, flogging, or crucifixion.

prominent Greeks had responded positively to the Gospel message. Consequently, the Thessalonian Jews turned some of the unbelieving Bereans against Paul, causing the Berean believers to escort Paul to Athens. Silas and Timothy stayed behind but later rejoined Paul in Athens and then still later in Corinth, causing Paul to travel alone to Athens. There is no further mention of Silas in the Acts narrative, but it seems likely that Silas continued to minister in Corinth after Paul left the city (Acts 18:5, 18). Paul mentions Silas in both 1 and 2 Thessalonians, and in 2 Corinthians 1:19. Silas served Peter as scribe and possibly deliverer and expositor of the epistle of 1 Peter to its recipients (1 Peter 5:12).

Timothy – Timothy was the son of a Greek father and a Jewish mother. His mother and grandmother – Eunice and Lois – were apparently strong believers and had taught Timothy the Scriptures well (2 Timothy 1:5; 3:14–15). It is likely that Timothy first met Paul and Barnabas in Lystra on their first missionary journey. He joined Paul and Silas on the second missionary journey, after being circumcised by Paul to avoid future misunderstandings. It is likely that he was still very young at this time because Paul later exhorts Timothy not to let others look down upon him due to his youth (1 Timothy 4:12). It appears that Timothy suffered from some form of chronic stomach illness (1 Timothy 5:23). It is remarkable to think that this young man served a newly planted church in Thessalonica after Paul was forced to leave! Timothy served in several other churches (see 1 Corinthians 4:17; Philippians 2:19), as well as in Ephesus (1 Timothy 1:3), where he was apparently imprisoned and later released (Hebrews 13:23). He later served as bishop of Ephesus until (tradition has it) he was clubbed to death by an angry mob in AD 97.[6] Timothy is mentioned in 1 and 2 Corinthians, Philippians, Colossians, 1 and 2 Thessalonians, and Philemon. Paul called him "my true son in the faith" (1 Timothy 1:2).

Titius Justus – Titius Justus was a God-fearer and lived next door to the synagogue in Corinth. He was probably a Roman citizen whose family had moved to Corinth during the time of Julius Caesar. There are variations in the spelling of his name in different Greek manuscripts, which is why he is often confused with Titus – Paul's co-worker, who was probably sent by Paul to Corinth later.

Crispus and his household – Crispus, a Corinthian Jew, was the ruler of the synagogue at Corinth. He, together with his household, believed the gospel and was baptized by Paul (1 Corinthians 1:14).

Barnabas – Barnabas was a Levite (Acts 4:36) whose family had moved to Cyprus. It is possible that he might have been a teacher of the law in a synagogue on that island. John Mark was his cousin (Colossians 4:10). His Jewish name was Joseph, but the apostles named him Barnabas, which means "son of encouragement" (Acts 4:36). Barnabas owned a piece of land – contrary to the Old Testament law (Joshua 13:33; 14:4)[7] – which he sold to alleviate the burden of those who were in need. According to Acts 9:27, it was Barnabas who recommended Paul to the apostles after Paul's return to Jerusalem from Damascus. When the church in Antioch began to grow cross-culturally, the

---

6. https://www.britannica.com/biography/Saint-Timothy.

7. It is possible that this was land within a Levitical city or part of the pastureland of the city (Leviticus 25:32; Jeremiah 32:6–8) or that this particular law was no longer observed after the restoration.

church in Jerusalem sent Barnabas to encourage the believers there, probably because Peter was already travelling. We are told that Barnabas was a righteous man, full of the Holy Spirit and faith (Acts 11:24). After being in Antioch for a while, Barnabas sought out Paul in Tarsus and brought him to Antioch to serve alongside him there (Acts 11:25–26). When the prophet Agabus predicted a great famine, the church in Antioch sent aid to the church in Jerusalem through Barnabas and Paul (Acts 11:27–30). Later, the Holy Spirit set apart Barnabas and Paul to take the gospel to the Gentiles (Acts 13:1–3), and they took with them John Mark (Acts 13:5b), who later left them in Perga and returned to Jerusalem (Acts 13:13). While ministering in Lystra, the local population mistook Barnabas for Zeus (Acts 14:12). Interestingly, Luke describes Barnabas as an apostle in Acts 14:14. Upon their return to Antioch, influenced by Peter's actions in the presence of Jewish believers from Jerusalem, Barnabas also began to avoid eating with the gentile believers (Galatians 2:11–14). Together with several other believers from Antioch, Barnabas accompanied Paul to attend the Jerusalem Council, where the matter of Gentile inclusion in the church was to be decided (Acts 15). Sometime later Paul decided to revisit the churches established in Galatia. Barnabas wanted to take along John Mark, his cousin, but Paul vehemently opposed this suggestion. As a result of this disagreement, Paul and Barnabas decided to go their separate ways, and John Mark accompanied Barnabas to Cyprus.

Barnabas is only mentioned once more in the Scriptures (1 Corinthians 9:5–6). Because of this positive reference to the ministry of Barnabas, some scholars assume that the two former co-workers had been reconciled at some point. The fact that John Mark served Paul while the apostle was a prisoner in Rome may indicate that Barnabas was no longer alive at that time (Colossians 4:10). According to Christian tradition, Barnabas was martyred at Salamis, and the Cypriot Orthodox Church claims him as their founder.

Peter – Simon Peter (also known as Cephas) and his brother Andrew were natives of Bethsaida but had, at some point, moved to Capernaum, where the brothers seemed to have set up a lucrative fishing business together with their partners – Zebedee and his sons, John and James. It is possible that the partners were related by marriage with Peter being married to Zebedee's daughter.[8] It is also possible that Zebedee's wife was Jesus's aunt, being the sister of Mary.[9] Peter first met Jesus through the witness of his brother Andrew, a former disciple of John the Baptist. Although Jesus changed his name from Cephas to Peter (John 1:42), the name Cephas was sometimes used by Paul (1 Corinthians 1:12; 3:21–22; 9:5; 15:5; Galatians 2:7–14). At first, Peter followed Jesus from a distance but soon took a leading role in the group, being chosen by Jesus as one of the inner circle of three. Despite his adamant protestations that he would defend Jesus to the death, at his master's trial, three times Peter denied that he was a follower of Jesus, a denial that he later rescinded by three affirmations of faith. After the ascension of Jesus, Peter assumed the leadership of the church in Jerusalem and was also one of the first to cross ethnic boundaries as a witness for Jesus (Acts 10). Church tradition

---

8. See Larry Helyer, *The Life and Witness of Peter*. Illinois: IVP Academic, 2012, 35.

9. John 19:25; see also Matthew 27:55; Mark 15:40. From these references to the women present at the cross it is possible to conclude that Salome, Zebedee's wife and mother of James and John, was the sister of Mary, mother of Jesus as well as the mother of Peter's wife. This would make Salome Jesus's aunt and James and John his cousins, which may explain why Jesus entrusted his mother to the care of John. But if Peter was married to Salome's daughter, then he would be cousin-in-law to Jesus. This all explains why Jesus, his mother, and his siblings could live together in Peter's compound in Capernaum.

claims that Peter established the church in Antioch and travelled to the churches in Cappadocia, Bithynia, Pontus, Galatia, and also Rome, where he is believed to have been martyred by Nero in AD 64 – crucified, upside down at his own request.[10]

James the brother of Jesus – James, Joseph, Simon, Judas, and their sisters were the children of Mary and Joseph and, therefore, half-siblings of Jesus (Matthew 13:55). James, like his siblings, is portrayed in the gospels as an unbeliever (John 7:2–5). However, he was one of the earliest witnesses of Jesus's resurrection (1 Corinthians 15:7). In his epistle, James identifies himself as "a servant of God and of the Lord Jesus Christ" (James 1:1). He never left Jerusalem and later became the leader of the church in that city. Together with Peter and Barnabas, he met with the recently converted Saul on his return to Jerusalem from Damascus (Galatians 1:19). At the Jerusalem Council, James was clearly the leader of the group (Acts 15:13, 19). Paul refers to James, Peter, and John as "esteemed pillars" of the early Christian community (Galatians 2:9). James also presided over a later meeting in Jerusalem where accusations against Paul – after his return following his third missionary journey – were dealt with (Acts 21:17–26). According to Josephus and several early church fathers, James was martyred in Jerusalem around AD 62.[11]

---

10. This is according to Orthodox tradition: "Church tradition maintains that the See of Antioch was founded by Saint Peter the Apostle in A.D. 34." https://saintignatiusbelfast.org/the-church-history-of-antioch. See also Eusebius, *Hist. eccl.* 2.9.1–4; 2.14.6, 15–16.

11. "This younger Ananus, who, as we have told you already, took the high priesthood, was a bold man in his temper, and very insolent; he was also of the sect of the Sadducees, who are very rigid in judging offenders, above all the rest of the Jews, as we have already observed; when, therefore, Ananus was of this disposition, he thought he had now a proper opportunity [to exercise his authority]. Festus was now dead, and Albinus was but upon the road; so he assembled the Sanhedrin of judges, and brought before them the brother

Judas, Barsabbas – In Acts 15:22, Judas Barsabbas and Silas are described as "leaders among the believers." These two men were chosen as delegates of the Council of Jerusalem and sent to accompany Paul and Barnabas to Antioch to deliver the Council's letter resolving the controversy regarding the inclusion of Gentiles in the church. Acts 15:32 states that Judas and Silas were "prophets" who greatly encouraged and strengthened the believers. They returned to Jerusalem (Acts 15:33), but Silas was later recalled to Antioch to accompany Paul on his second missionary journey (Acts 15:40).

Lucius of Cyrene – Lucius of Cyrene may have been one of the founding members of the church in Antioch (Acts 13:1). He was a member of the group that fasted and prayed and then commissioned Barnabas and Saul to take the gospel to Asia. He may have been one of the men from Cyrene who went to Antioch and began a cross-cultural ministry to Greek-speaking citizens (Acts 11:19–20). According to Orthodox church tradition, Lucius was appointed by John Mark to be the first bishop of Cyrene.[12]

Manaen – A teacher in the church at Antioch, Manaen is said to have been a lifelong friend of Herod Antipas (Acts 13:1). He

---

of Jesus, who was called Christ, whose name was James, and some others, [or, some of his companions]; and when he had formed an accusation against them as breakers of the law, he delivered them to be stoned." Josephus, *Ant.* 20:9:1. Quoting from Clement of Alexandria, Eusebius writes that "James was thrown from the pinnacle of the temple and was beaten to death with a club." Eusebius, *Hist. eccl.* II:23. He also quotes from Hegesippus, saying that "the Scribes and Pharisees placed James upon the pinnacle of the temple, and threw down the just man, and they began to stone him, for he was not killed by the fall. And one of them, who was a fuller, took the club with which he beat out clothes and struck the just man on the head." See https://en.wikisource.org/wiki/Nicene_and_Post-Nicene_Fathers:_Series_II/Volume_I/Church_History_of_Eusebius/Book_II/Chapter_23.

12. https://orthodoxwiki.org/Archdiocese_of_Cyrene.

was also a member of the group that commissioned Paul and Barnabas. Together with Lucius and Niger, he might have been one of the founding members of the church at Antioch. Manaen may have been a source for Luke's writings, providing details about Herod Antipas and other members of the Herodian family (Luke 3:1, 19–20; 8:3; 9:7–9; 13:31–32; 23:8–12; Acts 12). It is possible that Manaen was converted together with Joanna, the wife of Herod's steward Chuza (Luke 8:3), perhaps through the direct or indirect witness of the royal official from Capernaum whose son was healed by Jesus (John 4:46–54).

Simeon, Niger – Other than being mentioned as one of the prophets and teachers in the church in Antioch (Acts 13:1), very little is known about Simeon. It is possible that he was called "Niger" because he was of African descent.

John Mark – John, also known as Mark, was the son of a wealthy woman named Mary, who lived in Jerusalem (Acts 12:12). He was the cousin of Barnabas (Colossians 4:10; Philemon 24; 2 Timothy 4:11). John Mark accompanied Paul and Barnabas on their first missionary journey to Cyprus but left them in Perga and returned to Jerusalem. We do not know for certain what precipitated this departure, but it was of a sufficiently serious nature that Paul refused to take him along the second time. However, Barnabas took Mark with him to Cyprus. At some point, Paul was reconciled with both Barnabas (1 Corinthians 9:5–6) and John Mark (Colossians 4:10; Philemon 24; 2 Timothy 4:11). Quoting from Papias, Eusebius indicates that John Mark, in his capacity as Peter's student, scribe, or interpreter, wrote the Gospel of Mark.[13] According to tradition, John Mark was the founder of the church of Alexandria.[14]

Luke – Very little is known about the man whose two-volume work – the Gospel of Luke and the Acts of the Apostles – makes up about one quarter of the New Testament. Luke's authorship of this work is undisputed in the early church.[15] The abrupt change from the third person plural to the first person plural in the "we" passages as they are sometimes called (Acts 16:10–17; 20:5–16; 21:1–19; 27:1–28:16) indicates that the author is a participant in the events being described. Therefore, it seems plausible that the author was a personal eyewitness of these events and a companion of Paul on some of his journeys.[16] If this is the case, it appears that Luke first joined Paul, Silas, and Timothy in Troas (Acts 16:8–10) and travelled with them to Philippi, where he stayed behind for some reason, only meeting up with Paul again in Troas (Acts 20:5). Luke is described as a physician by Paul in Colossians 4:14, leading some scholars to believe that he might have been both a physician as well as a disciple of Paul. Many scholars believe that Luke was a Gentile man from Antioch, although others believe that he was either a Hellenistic Jew or a God-fearer, mainly because of his apparent extensive knowledge of the Septuagint – the Greek translation

---

13. Eusebius, *Hist. eccl.* 3.39.

14. "St. Mark the Apostle, the Founder of the Coptic Church," *Coptic Orthodox Answers*, 2016, https://copticorthodoxanswers.org/st-mark-founder-of-coptic-church/.

15. The Papyrus Bodmer XIV, which is the oldest known manuscript containing the ending of the gospel (dating to around AD 200), uses the superscription "The Gospel According to Luke." See also Irenaeus, *Haer.* 3.1.1, 3.14.1; Tertullian, *Marc.* 4.2.2; and Clement of Alexandria, *Paed.* 2.1.15 and *Strom.* 5.12.82 among others. No other ancient writers question Luke's authorship.

16. Irenaeus, *Haer.* 3.1.1.

of the Old Testament Scriptures. Epiphanius claims that Luke was one of the seventy disciples sent out by Jesus, an event that is only recorded in Luke 10.[17] From the quality of the Greek used in Luke and Acts, we may deduce that Luke was highly educated. He was obviously well schooled in ancient classical and hellenistic Greek since he quoted from or alluded to various Greek authors such as Homer, Aesop, Epimenides, Euripides, Plato, and Aratus. The first time Luke is mentioned by name is in Philemon 24. Paul also refers to him in Colossians 4:14 and 2 Timothy 4:11. Luke was with Paul in Rome during the apostle's first imprisonment in that city (Acts 28:11–16) and, according to 2 Timothy 4:11, was with him again during what appears to be a different imprisonment. Some traditions say that Luke died at the age of eighty-four in Boeotia, in Greece, while others claim that he was martyred in Rome shortly after the martyrdom of Peter and Paul.

Lydia – Lydia is only mentioned twice by name in Scripture (Acts 16:11–15, 40). She was a native of Thyatira but was living in Philippi when she met Paul during his second missionary journey. Thyatira was a centre of indigo trade, and Lydia is said to have been a seller of purple cloth, which may suggest that she had moved to Philippi to sell her wares there. As there is archaeological evidence of a dyers' guild in the city, Lydia might have been a member of this guild or might even have inaugurated such an association in Philippi. Acts 16:13–14 says that Lydia, together with a group of women, was worshipping God on the Sabbath at a place of prayer near a river outside Philippi. This may indicate, first, that Lydia was Jewish or a proselyte and, second, that there were not enough Jewish men in

---

17. Epiphanius, *Pan.* 51.11.

Philippi to form a synagogue.[18] Lydia believed and was baptized together with the other members of her household, which may have included not only her family but also household slaves. She insisted that the missionaries stay at her home while in Philippi. Lydia, although a native of Asia Minor, is the first recorded convert to Christianity in Europe. By the time the missionaries left Philippi, there seems to have been a group of believers – by that time, also including men – meeting in Lydia's home (Acts 16:40). It is interesting to note that by the time John wrote the book of Revelation, there was a sizeable church in Thyatira (Revelation 2:18–29). Since the Bible has no record of Paul or any other evangelist ever visiting Thyatira, it is possible that Lydia or one of her household brought the gospel to her hometown.

The slave girl and her owners – The slave girl, while unnamed, is said to have had the "spirit of python" that apparently enabled her to predict the future. Her owners capitalized on her abilities and were outraged when the exorcism robbed them of any further ill-gotten gains.[19]

The Philippian jailer and his household – It is possible that this unnamed jailor was a retired Roman soldier. The city of Philippi had been chartered as a "Roman Colonial City."

Jason and other believers – Jason (a Greek form of Joshua) played host to Paul, Silas, and Timothy for the duration of their

---

18. The minimum number of males required to constitute a representative "community of Israel" for liturgical purposes was ten. *Encyclopaedia Britannica Online*, "minyan," 2 February 2018. https://www.britannica.com/topic/minyan. See https://www.britannica.com/topic/minyan.

19. Megan Sauter, "Paul and the Slave Girl in Philippi," *Biblical Archaeology Society*, 18 April 2024, https://www.biblicalarchaeology.org/daily/people-cultures-in-the-bible/people-in-the-bible/paul-and-the-slave-girl-in-philippi/.

stay in Thessalonica. He was probably a Jew or a God-fearing Gentile who had heard Paul in the synagogue and believed in Jesus (Acts 17:4). He might have been prosperous since he not only hosted the group in his home but was also able to post bond not only for himself but also for Paul and Silas (Acts 17:9). The fact that Paul and Silas were forced out of Thessalonica leaving Jason to bear these legal costs might have given rise to the charge that Paul was a swindler who came to Thessalonica for personal gain – a charge that he dealt with in 1 Thessalonians 2:1–12. If the Jason mentioned in Romans 16:21 is the Jason of Thessalonica, then he was with Paul when the apostle wrote his letter to the church in Rome.

City Officials – In Acts 17:6 and 17:8, the city officials are called politarchs. This title has been verified by archaeologists, who have found it inscribed on various ruins in Thessalonica, one of which was the arch of the western entrance of the city known as the Vardar Gate.[20]

Berean believers – The Berean Jews, in contrast to the Thessalonian unbelieving Jews, are said to have been "more noble than those in Thessalonica; they received the word with all eagerness, examining the Scriptures daily to see if these things were so" (Acts 17:11 ESV). We may deduce from this that these Bereans were already in the habit of reading and

---

20. Marble building block from a Roman gateway at Thessalonika, with an inscription that lists civic officials: six Politarchs ('Rulers of the Citizens'), the Tamias (Treasurer) of the City, and the Gymnasiarch (Director of Higher Education), a graffito may also be present." https://www.britishmuseum.org/collection/object/G_1877-0511-1

Inscription translation: The politarchs are Sosipatros, son of Kleopatra and Lukios Pontius Secundus; Aulos Auios Sabeinos; Demetrios, son of Phaustos; Demetrios son of Neikopolis; Zoilos, son of Parmenion and of Meniskos; Gaios Agilleos Poteitos; the treasurer is Tauros, son of Ammia and of Reglos (i.e. Regulus); the gymnasiarch is Tauros, son of Tauros and Reglos.

studying the Scriptures daily and using the Scriptures as their standard of authority to verify information. As a result, these Jews were able to accept the truth of Paul's message about Jesus.

Epicurean and Stoic Philosophers – The Epicureans and Stoics were two popular Greek philosophical schools of thought. The Epicureans believed that pleasure within reason was the goal a person needed to pursue to achieve contentment because after this life, we simply cease to exist. "Since non-existence is our own inescapable destiny, we should make the best of the only life we have. The good life in this life, happiness in this world, should be our aim."[21] For this reason, Paul's teaching on the resurrection would have seemed ridiculous to them. The Stoics believed that there was nothing higher than or beyond this physical life and that since "nature itself is governed by rationally intelligible principles,"[22] humans should strive towards the development of self-control and submission to universal reason during this life. The Stoics categorized virtue into four main types: wisdom, justice, courage, and moderation. Like the Epicureans, the Stoics did not believe in immortality but taught that humans simply "dissolved back into nature."[23] The basic difference between these two schools of thought is that the Stoics sought to cultivate moral and ethical behaviour by living according to natural law, while the Epicureans sought to avoid any form of discomfort by seeking physical and essential gratification within the bounds of moderation.[24] The basic similarity between the two philosophies is that both sought to wrestle with the conundrum of suffering – if there was

---

21. Magee, *Story of Philosophy*, 45.

22. Magee, 46.

23. Magee, 46.

24. Stephen Hanselman, "Stoicism vs. Epicureanism," *Daily Stoic*, https://dailystoic.com/stoicism-vs-epicureanism/.

a God or even many gods, what was the point of suffering in this life? What was the point of any life after this life? So, to these groups, Paul's teaching about a saviour resembling a suffering servant who, through his death and resurrection, granted us eternal life would have sounded preposterous.

Dionysius – Dionysius the Areopagite is believed to have been an Athenian judge in Athens. Acts 17:34 says that he was converted through the preaching of Paul. According to tradition, Dionysius was either the first bishop of Athens or the second (after Hierotheus).

Damaris – Damaris (meaning "calf" or "heifer") is one of a small group of people who responded to Paul's teaching in Athens. Since she is mentioned by name, we may assume that she was either a prominent woman in Athens or that she was well known among those in the early church. It is possible, but not certain, that Damaris might have been the wife of Dionysius.

Gaius – Gaius was a Corinthian resident who responded to Paul's teaching and one of only a few people there (the others being Crispus and the household of Stephanas) who were baptized by Paul (1 Corinthians 1:14–16). Later, Gaius is mentioned as being one of Paul's travelling companions, along with Aristarchus (Acts 19:29). He is said to have been from Derbe and is included among the seven men who waited for Paul in Troas (Acts 20:4–5). In Romans 16:23, Gaius is described as having been host not just to Paul but to the whole church, possibly in Corinth. Some scholars think that the Gaius to whom the third Epistle of John is addressed may be the same man.

Stephanas – Stephanas, a member of the church at Corinth, was converted under Paul's ministry and baptized by him, along with his family. According to 1 Corinthians 16:17, it seems possible that Stephanas – along with Fortunatus and Achaicus – came to Ephesus from Corinth, bearing a letter from the Corinthians (1 Corinthians 7:1), to which Paul responded by writing 1 Corinthians. Concerning these three men, Paul says, "Now I urge you, brothers – you know that the household of Stephanas were the first converts in Achaia, and that they have devoted themselves to the service of the saints – be subject to such as these, and to every fellow worker and labourer. I rejoice at the coming of Stephanas and Fortunatus and Achaicus, because they have made up for your absence, for they refreshed my spirit as well as yours. Give recognition to such people" (1 Corinthians 16:15–18 ESV).

Phoebe – Phoebe seems to have been a prominent woman in Cenchreae. Paul describes her as the deacon of the church in that city, and he had entrusted her with the delivery of his letter to the Romans (Romans 16:1–2). For various reasons, some scholars believe that she might have been a wealthy patroness of Paul's ministry, and some suggest that since she travelled from Cenchreae to Rome, she was involved in the shipping industry, possibly even owning a fleet of ships.

Gallio – Junius Gallio, originally known as Lucius Annaeus Novatus, was born in Corduba, Baetica (Spain) around 5 BC. He was the elder brother of the Stoic philosopher and politician Lucius Annaeus Seneca. He assumed the name Gallio after being adopted by the senator Junius Gallio. He became proconsul of Achaia in AD 51 and is the Roman official who dismissed the charges brought by the Jews against Paul (Acts 18:12–17). Gallio's tenure was brief (AD 51–52) because ill-health compelled him to resign his post within a short period of time. According to Pliny, Gallio had to abandon his post for a sea voyage as a remedy for consumption.[25] It is possible that he was later sent, along with his brother, into exile on the island of Corsica, but it seems that they both returned to Rome in AD 49 when Seneca was selected to be tutor to the young Nero. After Nero forced Seneca to commit suicide, Gallio also took his own life in AD 65. A consul was one of the highest of the ordinary magistracies in the ancient Roman Republic.

Sosthenes – Acts 18:12–17 records that a man by the name of Sosthenes, the leader of the synagogue at Corinth – possibly succeeding Crispus – was beaten by a mob in the presence of the consul Gallio after Gallio had refused to proceed against Paul. The motives for the assault against Sosthenes are not known. Another man by the name of Sosthenes is mentioned in 1 Corinthians 1:1. If this refers to the same person, then Sosthenes had subsequently become a believer himself.

Places Mentioned

Achaia – Achaia was one of the major regions of Greece and often a battleground during conflicts between Greek city-states and foreign powers. In 146 BC, following the Roman conquest of Greece, Achaia became a Roman province. When compelled to leave Macedonia, Achaia seemed a logical destination for Paul since it would have been difficult for his persecutors to cross provincial boundaries to pursue him.

---

25. "In a discussion titled 'On the Medicinal use of seawater,' Pliny the Elder (AD c.23/4–79) recorded 'there being many other uses, the chief however being a sea voyage for those attacked by consumption, as I have said, and for haemoptysis, such as quite recently within our memory was taken by Annaeus Gallio after his consulship (post consulatum).'" Winter, "Rehabilitating Gallio," 297.

Antioch – The city was founded by Seleucus I Nicator and named after his father, Antiochus.[26] Situated at the foot of Mount Silpius, on the east bank of the Orontes River, a day's journey inland from Seleucia Pieria – its port – Antioch was strategically located at the juncture of several main trade routes. Many people groups, including Jews, had settled there, giving rise to a multiplicity of religions. Early church tradition states that Peter established the churches in Antioch in AD 34.[27] In AD 45, many Jews migrated to Antioch during the persecution recorded in Acts 11:19. Barnabas and Saul were sent out from Antioch on the first missionary journey around AD 46.

Areopagus – The Areopagus, also known as Mars Hill, is a prominent rocky limestone outcrop located north-west of the Acropolis in Athens. It served as a multifunctional site for both judicial and religious functions. Named after Ares, the Greek god of war, it was considered a sacred site.

Athens – Probably one of the most renowned cities of antiquity, Athens traces its history back to the Neolithic Age (6800–3200 BC). It rose to prominence in the fifth century BC as the centre of the Athenian Empire. As a leading city-state of Greece, it played an important role in the development of democracy, philosophy, and the arts. Although the city's power and influence waned after its defeat in the Peloponnesian War (431–404 BC), it remained a cultural and intellectual centre. Despite losing its political autonomy under Roman rule, Athens

---

26. "Although there were sixteen Antiochs in the ancient world – this and Pisidian Antioch are the only two mentioned in the Bible." Wilson, *Biblical Turkey*, 62.

27. Eusebius *Hist. Eccl.* 3.36. See also Origen, *Hom. Luc.* 4. Patrologia Graeca 13:1814 in Wikipedia, "Saint Peter," last revised 27 May 2024, https://en.wikipedia.org/wiki/Saint_Peter, and https://saintignatiusbelfast.org/the-church-history-of-antioch.

continued to attract scholars and philosophers because of its schools, libraries, and philosophical academies.

Berea – Founded by Macedonian settlers in the fourth century BC, Berea was considered somewhat remote as it was not situated along the Via Egnatia. The city was known for its religious tolerance.

Cenchreae – Located near Corinth, Cenchreae was an important port city located on the Saronic Gulf on the eastern coast of Achaia. Cenchreae had temples for Aphrodite, Asclepius, and Isis, as well as a large bronze image of Poseidon that was visible from the sea.

Corinth – Corinth was situated on a narrow stretch of land called an "isthmus" that connected mainland Greece with the Peloponnese peninsula and had two harbours on either end – Lechaion to the north-west and Cenchreae to the south-east. A paved road, over which boats could be hauled using wheeled platforms, linked the Aegean Sea with the Corinthian Gulf. This strategic position helped to make Corinth a very wealthy commercial city, attracting many entrepreneurs and traders from all over the Roman world. The city was also situated close to the famous town of Isthmia, where biennial games dedicated to the god Poseidon were held, attracting thousands of tourists, athletes, poets, and musicians. In 146 BC, the city was burned and levelled by the Roman general Lucius Mummius, leaving only a few survivors who lived among the ruins.[28] In 44 BC, Julius Caesar decided to make Corinth a Roman colony. Although he was assassinated on 15 March of the same year before he could carry out his plans, under his successor – Caesar Octavian (later Caesar Augustus) – Corinth

---

28. Nasrallah, *Archaeology*, 146.

was rebuilt as a Roman city, with Latin as its official language. In 27 BC, it was declared the seat of the provincial administration of Achaia. Other than the surviving indigenous population, the first inhabitants of Corinth were Roman veterans and emancipated slaves. The city was divided into colonists (the voting population) and resident aliens (the non-voting population). The colonists were further divided into tribes, with aristocrats being elected annually to serve in leadership positions and some also serving as priests in the imperial cult.[29] The city's development was so swift and its buildings so lavish that Corinth quickly surpassed Athens in both size and importance. Its agora was paved with marble and considered the largest in the empire, being even more expansive than the forum in Rome. In addition to the many gods of Greece and Rome, Corinth was also a centre of the imperial cult, boasting temples and statues throughout the city.

Cyprus – This is the third largest island in the Mediterranean. It is 222 kilometres long, 97 kilometres wide, and has mountains reaching a height of 1,007 metres. Salamis is the eastern port city where Paul, Barnabas, and John Mark landed after setting out from Antioch and travelling along the southern Roman road to Paphos, the provincial capital.[30]

Derbe – Derbe was a frontier town in the province of Galatia, situated on the border of eastern Lycaonia, about thirty kilometres from the road that led from the Cilician Gates to Iconium. Paul and Barnabas ended their first missionary journey here, but Paul returned there on his later trips (Acts 16:1; 18:23).[31]

---

29. Burnett, *Paul*, 226–27.
30. Wilson, *Biblical Turkey*, 113.
31. Wilson, *Biblical Turkey*, 151–54.

Ephesus – The major port city of Ephesus, located at the mouth of the Caister River, was founded in the tenth century BC by Greek settlers from Athens. During the Greek period, it flourished as a centre of culture, learning, and religious worship. It was also known for its magnificent Temple of Artemis. In 129 BC, Ephesus came under Roman rule and continued to thrive – both economically and culturally – becoming the capital of the Roman province of Asia. The city was renowned for its theatres, libraries, and public buildings and was also a centre for philosophy, magic, and medical studies.

Jerusalem – Jerusalem was an ancient city with a rich history. There is evidence of settlement dating back to around 4500 BC, and the city seems to have been a significant religious and political centre for various civilizations, including the Canaanites. Later, in the tenth century BC, it became the capital city of the kingdom of Judah under King David. David's successor, his son Solomon, built the First Temple, which was the central religious site of the Jewish people. However, in 586 BC, the Babylonians, under King Nebuchadnezzar II, conquered Jerusalem, destroyed the First Temple, and exiled many of the city's inhabitants. After the Babylonian captivity, Jerusalem, as well as a Second Temple, was gradually rebuilt, and, despite tensions with the rival Samaritan Temple on Mount Gerizim, the city slowly regained importance under Persian and Hellenistic rule. In 164 BC, the Maccabees defeated their Greek overlords, recaptured Jerusalem, cleansed the temple, and rededicated the altar. But by the time of Paul, Jerusalem was under Roman control, having been conquered by Pompey in 63 BC. The temple remained a significant religious centre, with the lavish Herodian-renovated Second Temple standing as the focal point of worship, which included pilgrimages for various festivals such as Passover.

Lystra – Located thirty-five kilometres south-west of Iconium, Lystra was colonized by Augustus in 25 BC as a military colony. Timothy, a man of mixed heritage (Acts 16:1, 3), who became a disciple and co-worker of Paul, was raised here by his Jewish grandmother Lois and his mother Eunice (2 Timothy 1:5).[32]

Macedonia – Although Macedonia's history dates back to the Archaic period (800–480 BC), it was under King Philip II in the fourth century BC that it rose to prominence. Philip's military reforms and diplomacy paved the way for the later expansions and conquests of his son, Alexander the Great. After Alexander's death, his empire was divided among his four generals. Antipater received Achaia and Macedonia, and he was succeeded, not long after, by his son, Cassander. The Roman victory in the Macedonian Wars (214–148 BC) led to the dissolution of the kingdom and its transformation into a Roman province in 146 BC. Macedonia flourished as an administrative and commercial province in the Roman Empire. Characterized by ethnical, cultural, and religious diversity, it also included a strong imperial cult.

Neapolis – Neapolis was an important port and commercial coastal city located on the eastern coast of Macedonia.

Paphos – Paphos lay on the south-western corner of Cyprus and served as an ancient trading port under the Greeks and Ptolemies of Egypt. By the time of Paul and Barnabas, however, it had become the capital of the new Roman province of Cyprus and was, therefore, the seat of the proconsul Sergius Paulus in AD 46 (Acts 13:7).

---

32. Wilson, 167–68.

Philippi – Philippi was a Roman colony and is described by Luke as "the leading city of that district of Macedonia" (Acts 16:12). It was originally established in 360 BC by Thasian colonists and called Crenides, but it was renamed by Philip II of Macedon in 356 BC after he found out that there was gold in the area. In 42 BC, Octavian (later known as Augustus Caesar) and Mark Anthony defeated the forces of Brutus and Cassias – two of Julius Caesar's assassins – in this area, after which Philippi was established as a Roman colony. As such, it was a blended city, with settlers and indigenous people living and worshipping side by side.

Pisidian Antioch – This city was situated at a height of 1236 metres and strategically located on an east-west road running from Ephesus to the Cilician Gates. Emperor Augustus used Pisidian Antioch as a military base. The city was linked to Perga by two roads, one of which was the Via Sebaste. While the central route was the most direct, it ascended precipitously through the steep Taurus Mountain gorges. Paul and Barnabas probably took the easier western route.[33]

Roman roads – The Romans built a network of over eighty-five thousand kilometres (fifty-three thousand miles) of well-constructed roads that connected various parts of the Roman Empire. These roads were designed for efficient transportation and communication, enabling the rapid movement of people, goods, and soldiers. These roads were typically paved with stone or gravel and were marked with milestones; and lodgings and waystations for travellers could be found along these roads. On his first missionary journey, Paul would have used the Via Sebaste to travel through Galatia. On his second missionary

---

33. Wilson, 96, 102–9.

journey, he would first have travelled along the Via Sebaste from Tarsus through the Cilician Gates to Derbe, Lystra, and Pisidian Antioch, and then probably left this major road to travel on to Troas. After having arrived in Macedonia, he would have travelled along the Via Egnatia from Philippi to Thessalonica, leaving it to go down to Berea and, later, to Athens and Corinth by sea. Paul would have used these same roads on the third missionary journey, but when he was taken to Rome as a prisoner, he would have travelled on the Via Appia after having landed at Puteoli.[34]

Salamis – Salamis was a significant city-state on the eastern coast of the island of Cyprus. It was renowned for its strategic location, maritime trade, and cultural significance, serving as a hub for Greek and Roman influences in the region. Besides its busy harbour, it possessed a sizeable amphitheatre, a stadium, and a well-equipped gymnasium – complete with cold and hot rooms, swimming pools and latrines, and Roman baths. Barnabas was a native of Cyprus (Acts 4:36–37) and may well have had family in the city.

Samothrace – Samothrace was a small mountainous island in the northern Aegean Sea and served as a convenient stopover for ships travelling from Asia to Macedonia. This island was an ancient mystery cult centre and the site of the sanctuary of the great gods.

The Taurus Mountains and the Cilician Gates – The Taurus Mountains are a rugged mountain range in what is now southern Turkey. They run parallel with the Mediterranean

---

34. Julian Spriggs, "Travel in the Roman Empire during the First Century," *Bringing God's Word to the Nations*, https://www.julianspriggs.co.uk/Pages/Travel.

coast and serve as a natural barrier separating the coastal plains from the Anatolian plateau. The Cilician Gates – located in the eastern part of the Taurus Mountains, just above Tarsus – was a narrow passageway through which a strategic route passed, effectively connecting the coast with the inland areas and facilitating trade and troop movement. Paul and Silas would have travelled along this road.

Thessalonica – Founded in 315 BC by Cassander, son of Antipater – who was one of Alexander the Great's generals – the city was named for Cassander's wife, Thessalonike, who was the daughter of Philip II and the half-sister of Alexander. Under Roman rule, Thessalonica flourished as a major commercial hub due to its strategic location on the Aegean Sea and its proximity to major trade routes. This city served as the capital of the Roman province of Macedonia. It was also a centre for Greek culture and learning and boasted impressive public buildings, theatres, and temples dedicated to a variety of gods. It was also known for its vibrant religious life, with a mix of Greek and Roman gods as well as a strong centre for the imperial cult.

Troas – Troas was a significant coastal port and commercial centre in the north-western region of what is now Turkey. This city was also known for its ethnic, cultural, and religious diversity. Paul met Luke in Troas. It was also here that Paul had the dream about a man asking him to come to Macedonia (Acts 16:8–9).

Timeline

AD 5?	Birth of Paul in Tarsus
AD 20?	Paul studies under Gamaliel II in Jerusalem
AD 33	Crucifixion, Resurrection, Ascension, Pentecost
AD 33	Jewish converts from different nations return home
AD 33–34	Jerusalem, Judea, and Samaria: Stephen martyred, Phillip's ministry
AD 34	Paul converted and goes to Arabia for three years
AD 34 (tradition)	Peter establishes the church in Antioch
AD 37	Paul returns to Damascus and escapes to Jerusalem
AD 37	Herod Agrippa I appointed king
AD 37	Paul with Peter
AD 37	Paul to Tarsus
AD 38	Peter heals Aeneas and Dorcas (Tabitha) and brings the gospel to Cornelius
AD 39–42 (tradition)	Peter travels to Caesarea, Antioch, Pontus, Galatia, Cappadocia, Asia, and Bithynia on to Rome

AD 41	Judea and Samaria added to Herod Agrippa's realm
AD 42/43	Barnabas goes to Antioch, summons Paul from Tarsus
AD 44	Peter returns to Jerusalem via Pontus, Bithynia, Galatia, Cappadocia, and Antioch
AD 44	The writing of 1 Peter
AD 44	Barnabas and Paul in Jerusalem with gifts of food from Antioch
AD 44	Execution of James the brother of John
AD 44	Imprisonment and escape of Peter
AD 44	Departure of the Twelve on international missions
AD 44	Death of Herod Agrippa I
AD 44–48	Barnabas, Paul, and John Mark to Antioch – first missionary journey
AD 48	Peter back to Jerusalem via Pontus, Bithynia, Galatia, Cappadocia, Asia, and Antioch
AD 48	Peter and Paul clash in Antioch
AD 48	Galatians
AD 49	Jerusalem Council
AD 49	Jews expelled from Rome
AD 49 (biblical/tradition)	Paul and Silas to Macedonia and Athens; Barnabas and Mark to Cyprus; Luke meets Paul in Troas and then stays on in Philippi

AD 50–52	Paul in Corinth; appears before Gallio, proconsul of Achaia
AD 51–52	1 Thessalonians
AD 51–52	2 Thessalonians
AD 52–53	Paul in Jerusalem and Antioch via Ephesus
AD 52–55	Third missionary journey – Paul in Ephesus
AD 53/54	1 Corinthians
AD 54	Nero becomes emperor
AD 55–56	Paul through Macedonia, Illyricum, and western Greece
c. AD 55–56	Philippians
c. AD 55–56	Philemon
c. AD 55–56	Colossians
c. AD 55–56	Ephesians
AD 56	2 Corinthians
AD 57	Paul in Corinth, Philippi, and Jerusalem
AD 57	Romans, from Corinth
AD 57–59	Paul imprisoned in Caesarea Maritima under Felix and Festus
AD 59	Paul shipwrecked on route to Rome
AD 60	Paul in Rome
AD 62?	Paul to Spain
AD 62–64	1 Timothy
AD 62–64	Titus

AD 62–64	2 Timothy
AD 62	James the brother of Jesus executed
AD 64	Fire in Rome
AD 64/65	Paul executed

Appendix

Peter wrote that there "are some things in (Paul's) letters that are hard to understand, which the ignorant and unstable twist to their own destruction."[1] To this day, readers of the letters to the Thessalonians continue to wrestle with Paul's eschatological references. As Craig Keener states, "The interpretations of this passage are more diverse than those of most passages in the New Testament."[2] Part of the problem is that we are starting from a point of disadvantage. We simply do not know what Paul told the Thessalonians while he was still with them.[3]

Scholars have highlighted various inconsistencies in the treatment of the topic of the end of the age in 1 and 2 Thessalonians as well as in other New Testament passages which speak about the second coming of Jesus. However, since my aim is to defend my interpretation of 2 Thessalonians 2:3–4, I will only refer to other passages as they relate to my reasoning. To begin with, one glaring difference between 1 Thessalonians 4:13–5:11 and 2 Thessalonians 2:1–12 is that in the former, there appear to be no signs as the Lord comes unexpectedly, like a thief, whereas in the latter, there appear to be clear signs indicating that the end is near – namely, the great apostasy and the revealing of "the man of lawlessness."

The various possible methods of resolving this and other apparent incongruities involve either suggesting that Paul's thinking or understanding changed between different letters being written, or the idea that some of the material was not

---

1. 2 Peter 3:16 ESV.
2. Keener, *IVP Background Commentary*, 596–597.
3. 2 Thessalonians 2:5.

written or authorised by Paul. However, both these approaches are incompatible with my understanding of biblical inspiration. The only other option open for us to explore is alternative exegesis or translation. Most scholars would agree that Paul is drawing from various passages in the Old Testament as well as from the teachings of Jesus, mainly referencing Matthew 24.

My understanding of Matthew 24 is as follows:

Matthew 24:1–2: Jesus's statement in response to the disciples' remarks about the temple.

Matthew 24:3: The disciples' two questions in response to Jesus's statement about the destruction of the temple: When will the temple be destroyed? When will the end of the age come?

Matthew 24:4–35: Jesus's answer to the first question (many specific and obvious signs).

Matthew 24:36–51: Jesus's answer to the second question (no signs whatsoever), beginning with a clear statement: "But concerning that day and hour no one knows, not even the angels of heaven, nor the Son, but the Father only" (24:36 ESV). This is in keeping with several New Testament passages that appear to indicate that the end of time will be unexpected and, therefore, unpredictable. Some of these passages are listed below, along with a brief description:

- Matthew 13:24–30: the parable of the wheat and the weeds that grow together in the kingdom until the end.
- Matthew 25:1–13: the parable of the wise and foolish virgins who did not know when the bridegroom would return.
- Mark 13:32: Jesus says that only the Father knows the time of the end.

- Luke 12:35–48: the need for readiness because the coming of the Son of Man is at an hour no one expects.
- Acts 1:7: Jesus clearly states that the time of the end is not for us to know.
- 2 Peter 3:10: the day of the Lord will come unannounced, like a thief.

These and other similar passages, including Paul's statements in 1 Thessalonians 5:1–11, seem to indicate that there will be no signs preceding the second coming of Jesus. If Paul was referencing Jesus's teaching on the subject in his second letter to the Thessalonians, then the great apostasy and the revealing of the man of lawlessness cannot be indicators of an imminent return of Jesus. Some scholars think that while Paul was referring to the second coming in 1 Thessalonians, he was referring to the destruction of Jerusalem in 2 Thessalonians, foretelling the desecration of the temple by Vespasian's soldiers in AD 70 as a result of the man of lawlessness taking his seat in the temple.[4]

While this might seem plausible, it makes me wonder what the destruction of Jerusalem would have meant to Gentiles in Thessalonica. How would that incident have comforted them? Perhaps those persecuting them were Jews and, therefore, if the Jews fell out of favour with the Roman Empire, it would bring an end to their persecution. Again, while this is possible, it does not seem as if Paul changed gears here, so to speak. He still appears to be addressing the same misunderstanding about the times and seasons that he deals with in his earlier letter (1 Thessalonians 4:17) in his opening remarks in chapter 2 of

---

4. Keener, *IVP Background Commentary*, 596–97.

his second letter: "Concerning the coming of our Lord Jesus Christ and our being gathered to him" (2 Thessalonians 2:1).

As I write about Paul, I try to think about what might have been going on in the thoughts of a man who had dedicated the first half of his life to the study of the Torah, the Writings, and the Prophets to a degree where he could say he excelled beyond even his teachers. The major theme of the Old Testament seems to be deliverance – starting with God's promise in Genesis 3:15, moving through the events of the exodus, the period of the judges and kings, the restoration after the exile, and ending with a Messianic expectation. The Old Testament authors, like the New Testament authors, often had to deal with unfulfilled expectations due to delayed deliverance.

As I considered the passage in 2 Thessalonians 2:1–12, what came to mind was the statement God made to Abraham in Genesis 15:16 regarding the deliverance from bondage in Egypt being delayed until the iniquity of the Amorites had passed a grace period, and I wondered if there was perhaps a connection between the period of delay in the exodus event and the period of delay in the *parousia*. Paul seemed to have had in mind an extended grace period coming to an end when he wrote of the unbelieving Jews who "heap up their sins to the limit" (1 Thessalonians 2:16 NIV) to the point where God's judgement was inevitable and unavoidable. In 1 Thessalonians 2:16 I do believe Paul had the destruction of Jerusalem in mind.[5]

If Paul applied that same thought to the "delay" in Jesus's return, then perhaps the apostasy, the man of lawlessness, and the agent of restraint address a point in time when the grace period is terminated, like the sins of the Amorites (Genesis 15:6) or the sins of the unbelieving Jews (1 Thessalonians 2:16).

---

5. A similar denouncement is made in 2 Kings 21:10–16 and 23:26–27 regarding the sins of Manasseh.

Just as in the time of Noah lawless humanity continued in their apostasy or rebellion until the day God closed the ark, similarly, the evildoer will still do evil, and the filthy will still be filthy, and the righteous will still do right, and the holy will still be holy (Revelation 22:11) until the time is right for the end of the age and the return of Jesus. This corresponds with the parable of the wheat and the weeds and the parable of the wise and foolish virgins, as well as with the Lord's repeated warnings for us to be vigilant because his coming would be unexpected, warnings that come with statements about ongoing aspects of rebellion as well. To me, this idea of deferred eschatology based on a period of grace seems to align well with Paul's teaching in these two letters.

For this reason, I have chosen to translate 2 Thessalonians 2:3-4 in general rather than in specific terms. In other words, rather than have Paul pointing to a specific person, I have him pointing to a collective lawlessness that is currently being restrained by God until such a time when the rebellion reaches a point of no return. Then, just as God promised Abraham that his people would be delivered after the sins of the Amorites had gone beyond the grace period (Genesis 15:16), the sins of humanity will continue beyond the period of grace and the Lord will return to consummate his kingdom.

Bibliography

Bandy, Alan S. *An Illustrated Guide to the Apostle Paul: His Life, Ministry, and Missionary Journeys*. Grand Rapids: Baker Books, 2021.

Barclay, John M. G. "Conflict in Thessalonica." *The Catholic Biblical Quarterly* 55, no. 3 (July 1993): 512–530.

———. *Paul and the Power of Grace*. Grand Rapids: Eerdmans, 2020.

———. *Paul: A Very Brief History*. London: SPCK, 2017.

———. *Pauline Churches and Diaspora Jews*. Grand Rapids: Eerdmans, 2016.

Barnett, Paul. *Jesus and the Rise of Early Christianity: A History of New Testament Times*. Downers Grove: InterVarsity Press, 1999.

Beale, G. K. *1–2 Thessalonians*. Volume 13 in The IVP New Testament Commentary Series. Downers Grove: IVP Academic, 2003.

Bijl, Johannes W. H. van der. *For the Life of the World: The Multiplication of Simon Peter*. Carlisle: Langham Preaching Resources, 2022.

———. *Galatians: A Life in Letters*. Carlisle: Langham Global Library, 2024.

Bomar, David, ed. *Journeys of the Apostle Paul*. Bellingham: Lexham, 2019.

Bruce, F. F. *The Acts of the Apostles: The Greek Text with Introduction and Commentary*. Leicester: Inter-Varsity Press, 1976.

———. *Paul: Apostle of the Heart Set Free*. Grand Rapids: Eerdmans, 1977.

Burnett, D. Clint. *Paul and Imperial Divine Honors: Christ, Caesar, and the Gospel*. Grand Rapids: Eerdmans, 2024.

Chalke, Steve. *The Lost Message of Paul*. London: SPCK, 2019.

Constantineanu, Corneliu, ed. *Central and Eastern European Bible Commentary*. Carlisle: Langham Global Library, 2022.

Edson, Charles. "Cults of Thessalonica (Macedonica III)." *Harvard Theological Review* 41, no. 3 (July 1948): 153–204.

Farrow, Douglas. *1 & 2 Thessalonians*. Brazos Theological Commentary on the Bible. Grand Rapids: Brazos, 2020.

Flemming, Dean. *Contextualization in the New Testament: Patterns for Theology and Mission*. Downers Grove: IVP Academic, 2005.

Gardner, Joseph L. *Who's Who in the Bible: An Illustrated Biographical Dictionary*. New York: Reader's Digest, 1994.

Garland, David E. *1 Corinthians*. Baker Exegetical Commentary on the New Testament. Grand Rapids: Baker Academic, 2003.

Gorman, Michael J. *Cruciformity: Paul's Narrative Spirituality of the Cross*. Grand Rapids: Eerdmans, 2001.

———. *Reading Paul*. Eugene: Cascade Books, 2008.

Gupta, Nijay K. "The Thessalonian Believers, Formerly 'Pagans' or 'God-Fearers'?: Challenging a Stubborn Consensus." *Neotestamentica* 52, no. 1 (2018): 91–114.

Harvey, John D. *Listening to the Text: Oral Patterning in Paul's Letters*. Grand Rapids: Baker Books, 1998.

Hays, Richard B. *Echoes of Scripture in the Letters of Paul*. New Haven: Yale University Press, 1989.

Jeffers, James S. *The Greco-Roman World of the New Testament Era: Exploring the Background of Early Christianity*. Downers Grove: InterVarsity Press, 1999.

Keener, Craig S. *Acts: An Exegetical Commentary*. Grand Rapids: Baker Academic, 2014.

———. *The IVP Bible Background Commentary*. 2nd ed. Downers Grove: InterVarsity Press, 2014.

Koehler, Paul F. *Telling God's Stories with Power: Biblical Storytelling in Oral Cultures*. Pasadena: William Carey, 2010.

Koudougueret, Rosalie. "2 Thessalonians." In *The Africa Bible Commentary*, edited by Tokunboh Adeyemo. Nairobi: Word Alive Publishers, 2006.

Longenecker, Richard N. *The Acts of the Apostles*. Vol. 9 of *The Expositor's Bible Commentary*. Grand Rapids: Zondervan, 1981.

Louw, Johannes P., and Eugene A. Nida, eds. *Greek-English Lexicon of the New Testament Based on Semantic Domains*. 2nd ed. Vols. 1 and 2. New York: United Bible Societies, 1989.

Magee, Bryan. *The Story of Philosophy: A Concise Introduction to the World's Greatest Thinkers and Their Ideas*. New York: DK Publishing, 1998.

McKee, J. K. *1&2 Thessalonians: For the Practical Messianic*. McKinney: Messianic Apologetics, 2012.

McKnight, Scot. *Philippians and 1&2 Thessalonians*. Grand Rapids: Harper Christian Resources, 2022.

McKnight, Scot, and B. J. Oropeza. *Perspectives on Paul: Five Views*. Grand Rapids: Baker Academic, 2020.

Mee, Christopher, and Antony Spawforth. *Greece: An Oxford Archaeological Guide*. Oxford: Oxford University Press, 2004.

Moo, Douglas J. *A Theology of Paul and His Letters. Biblical Theology of the New Testament*. Grand Rapids: Zondervan, 2021.

Nanos, Mark D. *Reading Paul within Judaism*. Vol. 1 of *Collected Essays of Mark D. Nanos*. Eugene: Cascade Books, 2017.

Nasrallah, Laura Salah. *Archaeology and the Letters of Paul*. Oxford: Oxford University Press, 2019.

Peterman, G. W. *Paul's Gift from Philippi: Conventions of Gift Exchange and Christian Giving*. Society for New Testament Studies Monograph Series 92. Cambridge: Cambridge University Press, 1997.

Sampley, J. Paul. "The First Letter to the Corinthians," In volume 10 of *The New Interpreter's Bible: A Commentary in Twelve Volumes*. Nashville: Abingdon, 2002.

Schnabel, Eckhard J. *Early Christian Mission: Paul and the Early Church*. Downers Grove: IVP Academic, 2004.

Schreiner, Thomas R. *Interpreting the Pauline Epistles*. 2nd ed. Grand Rapids: Baker Academic, 2011.

Shogren, Gary S. *1 & 2 Thessalonians*. Grand Rapids: Zondervan Academic, 2012.

Smith, Abraham. "The Second Letter to the Thessalonians." In volume 11 of *The New Interpreter's Bible: A Commentary in Twelve Volumes*. Nashville: Abingdon, 2000.

Stewart, James S. *A Man in Christ: The Vital Elements of St. Paul's Religion*. Pantianos Classics, 1935.

Stott, John R. W. *The Message of Acts: The Spirit, the Church and the World*. The Bible Speaks Today. Downers Grove: InterVarsity Press, 1990.

Taylor, N. H. "Who Persecuted the Thessalonian Christians?" *HTS Teologiese Studies/Theological Studies* 58, no. 2 (2002).

Tsevas, Costas. *Greece: A Biblical Tour of Greek Historical Sites*. Chattanooga: AMG, 2022.

Valdez, Erbey Galvan. *On the Shores of Perga: How John Mark's Departure from the First Pauline Missionary Journey Changed the Gentile World*. Bloomington: WestBow, 2020.

Wagner, C. Peter. *The Book of Acts: A Commentary*. Ventura: Regal, 2008.

Walker, Peter. *In the Steps of Saint Paul: An Illustrated Guide to Paul's Journeys*. Oxford: Lion Hudson, 2011.

Wall, Robert W. "The Acts of the Apostles." In volume 10 of *The New Interpreter's Bible: A Commentary in Twelve Volumes*. Nashville: Abingdon, 2002.

Wangerin, Walter, Jr. *Paul: A Novel*. Grand Rapids: Zondervan, 2000.

Weima, Jeffrey A. D. *1-2 Thessalonians*. Baker Exegetical Commentary on the New Testament. Grand Rapids: Baker Academic, 2014.

———. "Infants, Nursing Mother, and Father: Paul's Portrayal of a Pastor." *Calvin Theological Journal* 37 (2002): 209-29.

Wilson, Mark. *Biblical Turkey: A Guide to the Jewish and Christian Sites of Asia Minor*. Istanbul: Ege Yayinlari, 2020.

Winter, Bruce W. *After Paul Left Corinth: The Influence of Secular Ethics and Social Change*. Grand Rapids: Eerdmans, 2001.

———. "Rehabilitating Gallio and His Judgement in Acts 18:14-15." *Tyndale Bulletin* 57, no. 2 (2006): 291-308.

Witherington, Ben, III. *1 and 2 Thessalonians: A Socio-Rhetorical Commentary*. Grand Rapids: Eerdmans, 2006.

Wright, N. T. *Jesus and the Victory of God*. Minneapolis: Fortress, 1996.

———. *Paul: A Biography*. London: SPCK, 2018.

———. *Paul and the Faithfulness of God*. Parts I-IV. Minneapolis: Fortress Press, 2013.

———. *Paul for Everyone: Galatians and Thessalonians*. London: SPCK, 2004.

———. *The Resurrection of the Son of God*. Minneapolis: Fortress, 2003.

Bibles Consulted

Africa Study Bible. Edited by John Jsu. Oasis International, 2016.

The Greek New Testament, 3rd edition. Edited by Kurt Aland, Matthew Black, Carlo M. Martini, Bruce M. Metzger, and Allen Wikgren. Stuttgart: United Bible Societies, 1983.

The Interlinear Bible. Edited by Jay P. Green. Grand Rapids: Baker Book House, 1985.

The Jerusalem Bible: Reader's Edition. New York: Doubleday, 1968.

JPS Hebrew-English Tanakh: The Traditional Hebrew Text and the New JPS Translation. 2nd ed. Philadelphia: Jewish Publication Society, 2000.

NIV Archaeological Study Bible. Grand Rapids: Zondervan, 2005.

NRSV Cultural Backgrounds Study Bible: Bringing to Life the Ancient World of Scripture. Edited by Keener Walton. Grand Rapids: Zondervan, 2019.

The Passion Translation. Edited by Brian Simmons. BroadStreet Publishing Group, 2018.

A Reader's Hebrew and Greek Bible. Edited by Richard J. Goodrich, Albert J. Lukaszewski, Philip A. Brown, and Bryan W. Smith. Grand Rapids: Zondervan, 2008.

Langham Literature and its imprints are a ministry of Langham Partnership.

Langham Partnership is a global fellowship working in pursuit of the vision God entrusted to its founder John Stott –

> ***to facilitate the growth of the church in maturity and Christ-likeness through raising the standards of biblical preaching and teaching.***

Our vision is to see churches in the Majority World equipped for mission and growing to maturity in Christ through the ministry of pastors and leaders who believe, teach and live by the word of God.

Our mission is to strengthen the ministry of the word of God through:
- nurturing national movements for biblical preaching
- fostering the creation and distribution of evangelical literature
- enhancing evangelical theological education

especially in countries where churches are under-resourced.

Our ministry

Langham Preaching partners with national leaders to nurture indigenous biblical preaching movements for pastors and lay preachers all around the world. With the support of a team of trainers from many countries, a multi-level programme of seminars provides practical training, and is followed by a programme for training local facilitators. Local preachers' groups and national and regional networks ensure continuity and ongoing development, seeking to build vigorous movements committed to Bible exposition.

Langham Literature provides Majority World preachers, scholars and seminary libraries with evangelical books and electronic resources through publishing and distribution, grants and discounts. The programme also fosters the creation of indigenous evangelical books in many languages, through writer's grants, strengthening local evangelical publishing houses, and investment in major regional literature projects, such as one volume Bible commentaries like *The Africa Bible Commentary* and *The South Asia Bible Commentary*.

Langham Scholars provides financial support for evangelical doctoral students from the Majority World so that, when they return home, they may train pastors and other Christian leaders with sound, biblical and theological teaching. This programme equips those who equip others. Langham Scholars also works in partnership with Majority World seminaries in strengthening evangelical theological education. A growing number of Langham Scholars study in high quality doctoral programmes in the Majority World itself. As well as teaching the next generation of pastors, graduated Langham Scholars exercise significant influence through their writing and leadership.

To learn more about Langham Partnership and the work we do visit
langham.org